PREPARING TO GO SHOPPING

In addition to vocabulary and the story, the activities for this chapter focus on:
1. relative clauses and their antecedents.
2. the forms of the relative pronoun.
3. the gender, case, and number of relative pronouns in their clauses.

Vocabulary

Activity 28a Vocabulary

Study the vocabulary list on page 195 alone or with a partner.

The Story and Building the Meaning

Relative Clauses I

Activity 28b Vocabulary in Context

Fill in the blanks to match the English cues.

1. Phrygia et Syra, quae _____ Aurēliae _____ cūrābant, dominam vexābant. (hair) (carelessly)

2. Syra, _____ manus tremēbat, dominam nōn bene cūrāre poterat. (whose)

3. Aurēlia, neglegentiā ancillārum _____, "Abīte!" clāmāvit. (annoyed)

4. Aurēlia in animō habēbat īre ad tabernam mercātōris cuiusdam, quī _____

   optimōs _____ solēbat. (dormice) (to sell)

5. Servī, quōs Aurēlia iussit _____ ad iānuam ferre, mātrem et fīliam ad tabernam mercātōris portābunt. (sedan chairs)

6. Servus iam ēmit _____, quem domum tulit. (a pig)

Forms

Relative Pronouns

Activity 28c Relative Pronouns: Endings and Forms

Next to each of the relative pronouns below, write the number of the declension (1st, 2nd, or 3rd) that has the same ending for that gender, case, and number. Then fill in the missing forms of the relative pronoun.

	Masculine	Singular Feminine	Neuter
Nom.	_____	_____	_____
Gen.	_____	_____	_____
Dat.	_____	_____	_____
Acc.	quem _____	quam _____	_____
Abl.	quō _____	quā _____	quō _____

	Masculine	Plural Feminine	Neuter
Nom.	quī _____	quae _____	_____
Gen.	quōrum _____	quārum _____	quōrum _____
Dat.	quibus _____	quibus _____	quibus _____
Acc.	quōs _____	quās _____	_____
Abl.	quibus _____	quibus _____	quibus _____

Building the Meaning

Relative Clauses II

Activity 28d The Function of the Relative Pronoun in Its Clause

- a. Underline the relative clauses in the following sentences.
- b. Circle the antecedents.
- c. Give the gender and number of the relative pronoun and its antecedent.
- d. Give the case of the relative pronoun and its function in its clause.
- e. Then translate the sentence:

1. Speculum, quod Syra nōn bene tenet, novum est.

Gender and number of the relative pronoun and its antecedent: _____
_____

Case of the relative pronoun and its function in its clause: _____
_____

Translation: _____
_____

2. Ancilla, quae crīnēs Aurēliae neglegenter pectēbat, erat Phrygia.

Gender and number of the relative pronoun and its antecedent: _____
_____

Case of the relative pronoun and its function in its clause: _____
_____

Translation: _____
_____

3. Māter fīliam, quae iam in cubiculō suō dormit, in urbem dūcere vult.

Gender and number of the relative pronoun and its antecedent: _____
_____

Case of the relative pronoun and its function in its clause: _____
_____

Translation: _____
_____

4. Amīcī, ad quōs Cornēlius nūntium mīsit, ad cēnam tribus diēbus advenient.

Gender and number of the relative pronoun and its antecedent: _____
_____

Case of the relative pronoun and its function in its clause: _____
_____

Translation: _____
_____

5. Taberna, in quā Aurēlia glīrēs optimōs invēnit, nōn procul aberat.

Gender and number of the relative pronoun and its antecedent: _____

_____

Case of the relative pronoun and its function in its clause: _____

_____

Translation: _____

_____

6. Servī, quōs Aurēlia vocāverat, duās sellās ad iānuam celeriter tulērunt.

Gender and number of the relative pronoun and its antecedent: _____

_____

Case of the relative pronoun and its function in its clause: _____

_____

Translation: _____

_____

Activity 28e Combining Sentences Using a Relative Pronoun

Combine the following pairs of sentences by changing the second into a relative clause and inserting it into the first sentence. In every case you will substitute a relative pronoun for the word in boldface. Your new Latin sentence should match the English translation given below. The first set is done for you.

1. Aurēliae crīnēs pulchrī erant.

Duae ancillae **crīnēs** pectēbant.

Aurēliae crīnēs, quōs duae ancillae pectēbant, pulchrī erant. _____

Aurelia's hair, which two slave-women were combing, was pretty.

2. Mercātor glīrēs optimōs vēndere solet.

Taberna **mercātōris** est prope Forum.

_____

The merchant, whose shop is near the Forum, is accustomed to selling excellent dormice.

3. Phrygia Cornēliam vocāvit.

   Cornēlia in hortō librum legēbat.

   _____

   Phrygia called Cornelia, who was reading a book in the garden.

4. Sella erat nova.

   Sellam servī fortēs ad iānuam ferēbant.

   _____

   The sedan chair, which strong slaves were carrying to the door, was new.

5. Cornēlius amīcōs ad cēnam invītāvit.

   Amīcī erant senātōrēs Rōmānī.

   _____

   Cornelius invited friends, who were Roman senators, to dinner.

Applying What You Have Learned

Activity 28f Writing the Language

Translate the following English sentences into Latin. Include all long marks. Use the story and vocabulary lists in your textbook, as well as the vocabulary lists in this book, to help you:

1. Those two slave-women, who will help Aurelia again tomorrow, are anxious.

   _____

   _____

2. Eucleides will be reading that new book that he bought yesterday.

   _____

   _____

3. Aurelia, who is sometimes an anxious mistress, will be busy in the kitchen.

   _____

   _____

4. For what reason? Her husband, who is a distinguished senator, has invited certain friends to dinner.

_____

_____

5. The dinner that Aurelia will prepare in three days ought to be very good.

_____

_____

Activity 28g Expanding Your English Vocabulary

Using the word bank below, write the word that could replace the italicized word or words in each sentence. Use the Latin words in parentheses to help determine the meaning of the English words. Then write the English translation of each Latin word in the word bank:

1. Aurelia is annoyed by Phrygia's *carelessness*.   _____

2. Aurelia finds Syra's behavior very *annoying*.   _____

3. Many *sellers* gather in the Forum to display their goods.   _____

4. A large man with a *pig-like* face was sitting in a sedan chair.   _____

5. Of all the goddesses, Venus was best known for her *beauty*.   _____

porcine **(porcus)** _____	pulchritude **(pulcher)** _____
vexatious **(vexāre)** _____	vendors **(vēndere)** _____
negligence **(neglegenter)** _____	

Activity 28h Reading Latin

In the Kitchen

*Look at the new vocabulary following this story. Then read the story, noting the relative clauses and words beginning with **qu-** or **cui-**. Reread the story for comprehension. Then mark whether each statement about the story is V = **Vērum** (True) or F = **Falsum** (False):*

Postquam Cornēlia et Aurēlia in sellīs discessērunt, Elissa, ancilla nova, cum aliīs ancillīs in culīnā strēnuē labōrābat.

Syra:	Ubi tū antehāc habitāvistī, Elissa?
Elissa:	Habitābām apud familiām, cuius vīlla extrā urbem in collibus est. Ēheu! Vīlla nostra erat magna, sed nōn erant multī servī. Cotīdiē strenuē labōrāre necesse erat. Quam miserī erāmus!
Syra:	Quam fēlīx nunc es! Certē domus Cornēliī magna est, sed dominus noster multōs servōs et multās ancillās habet. Cūrāmus bonam familiam, quae nūper ad urbem subitō rediit.
Anna:	Habēmus duōs strenuōs puerōs, Mārcum et Sextum, quibus multum cibum parāmus quod semper ēsuriunt! Mārcus est fīlius dominī nostrī et puer optimus.
Elissa:	Quis est Sextus?
Anna:	Pater Sextī, quem prīnceps ad Asiam mīsit, est hospes Cornēliī. Sextus igitur cum familiā nostrā manet. Sunt in urbe multa quae Sextus numquam anteā vīdit.
Elissa:	Quid est nōmen fīliae, quam in sellā vīdī? Cūr cum mātre suā discessit?
Anna:	Cornēlia est fīlia Aurēliae, quācum ad tabernās iit. Glīrēs et multa alia ement.
Elissa:	Quam ob causam glīrēs ement? Quam ob causam tantus strepitus in domō est? Cūr omnēs strēnuē labōrāmus?

(Subitō intrāvit Phrygia sollicita, quae omnia audīverat.)

Phrygia:	Cornēlius, dominus noster, habet amīcōs, quōs ad cēnam invītāvit. Tribus diēbus convīvae advenient. Nōbīs igitur cibum coquere et domum parāre necesse est. Ātrium pūrgāre vōbīs necesse est, Syra et Elissa. Holera parāre tibi necesse est, Anna. Vestra neglegentia dominam valdē vexābit. Agite, ignāvae ancillae! Tempus est strēnuē labōrāre!

antehāc, adv., *previously*
collis, collis, m., *hill*
fēlīx, fēlīcis, *happy, lucky*

nūper, adv., *recently*
emō, emere, ēmī, ēmptus, *to buy*
convīva, -ae, m., *guest*
holus, holeris, n., *vegetable*

1. Elissa extrā urbem in collibus habitābat.   V   F

2. Cornēliī habitant in domō in quā nōn sunt multī servī et multae ancillae.   V   F

3. Ancillae cūrant Cornēliōs quī ad urbem nūper rediērunt.   V   F

4. Puerī multum cibum ancillīs parant.   V   F

5. Prīnceps Cornēlium ad Asiam mīsit.   V   F

6. Nōmen puellae quae in sellā discessit Cornēlia est.   V   F

7. Syra et Elissa holera parābunt; Anna ātrium pūrgābit.   V   F

GOING TO THE MARKET

Go Online
PHSchool.com
Web Code: jgd-0002

In addition to vocabulary and the story, the activities for this chapter focus on:
1. relative pronouns.
2. words beginning with **qu-**.
3. the indefinite adjective **quīdam, quaedam, quoddam**.
4. the interrogative pronoun **Quis…? Quis…? Quid…?**

Vocabulary

Activity 29a Vocabulary

Study the vocabulary list on page 196 alone or with a partner. Go to the corresponding list on the Companion website where you will find the six **qu-** *words given on pages 13–14 of your textbook.*

The Story

Activity 29b Questions on the Story

Complete the answers to these questions based on the story in Chapter 29:

1. Quī Aurēliam et Cornēliam per urbem ferēbant?

   _____ Aurēliam et Cornēliam per urbem ferēbant.

2. Quī onera ingentia portābant?

   _____ onera ingentia portābant.

3. Quae rēs Cornēliam dēlectant?

   _____ eam dēlectant.

4. Quid mendīcī petunt?

   _____ mendīcī petunt.

5. Quī lectīcam hominis obēsī portant?

   _____ lectīcam hominis obēsī portant.

6. Quid homō obēsus in manū habet?

   _____ homō obēsus in manū habet.

7. Cuius ē manibus effugit porcus?

_____ effugit porcus.

8. Quis in lutum propter porcum fugientem cadit?

_____ in lutum propter porcum fugientem cadit.

9. Quī homō est īrā commōtus?

_____ est īrā commōtus.

10. Ubi Cornēlia et Aurēlia dē sellīs dēscendērunt?

_____ Cornēlia et Aurēlia dē sellīs dēscendērunt.

Relative Pronouns

Activity 29c Relative Pronouns

Insert the correct form of the relative pronoun to complete these sentences.

1. Servī, _____ sellās portābant, fortēs erant.

2. Sellae, _____ servī portābant, magnae erant.

3. Onera, _____ servī in viīs portābant, ingentia erant.

4. Domina, _____ sellam servī portābant, uxor senātōris erat.

5. Taberna, in _____ Aurēlia glīrēs emet, in Forō Boāriō est.

6. Viae, in _____ multī servī currēbant, plēnae hominum erant.

7. Poētae, _____ Cornēlia cōnspexit, versūs recitābant.

8. Subitō porcus, _____ servus quīdam portābat, ē manibus servī effūgit.

9. Mercātor, _____ Aurēlia pecūniam dederit, laetus erit.

10. Taberna, _____ māter et fīlia petunt, nōn procul abest.

Activity 29d Combining Sentences Using a Relative Pronoun

Combine the following pairs of sentences by changing the second into a relative clause and inserting it into the first sentence. In every case you will substitute a relative pronoun for the word in boldface. Your new Latin sentence should match the English translation given below.

1. Vehiculum ingēns erat.

   Vehiculum onus portābat.

   _____

   The vehicle, which was carrying a load, was huge.

2. Cornēlia poētam cōnspicit.

   Poēta versūs recitat.

   _____

   Cornelia catches sight of a poet, who is reciting verses.

3. Cornēlia lectīcam ēlegantissimam videt.

   Homō in **lectīcā** recumbit.

   _____

   Cornelia sees a very elegant litter, in which a man is reclining.

4. Homō īrātus est.

   Hominī porcus currēns nocet.

   _____

   The man, whom the running pig harms, is angry.

Building the Meaning

Activity 29e Common Words Beginning with *qu-*

*Complete these Latin sentences by writing the correct form of one of the words beginning with **qu-** on the line at the left. Then identify the **qu-** word by writing one of the following numbers on the line at the right:*

   1. a relative pronoun, **quī, quae, quod**
   2. an indefinite adjective, **quīdam, quaedam, quoddam**

3. an interrogative pronoun, **Quis...? Quis...? Quid...?**
4. the causal conjunction, **quod**
5. the exclamatory adverb, **Quam...!**
6. an interrogative adjective, **Quī...? Quae...? Quod...?**

1. Who was combing Aurelia's hair?

_____ crīnēs Aurēliae pectēbat?   _____

2. How angry Aurelia is!

_____ īrāta est Aurēlia!   _____

3. Whom did Cornelia see in the city?

_____ in urbe vīdit Cornēlia?   _____

4. She saw a certain poet reciting verses.

Poētam _____ versūs recitantem vīdit.   _____

5. Aurelia arrived at the shop of the merchant, who sold the best dormice.

Aurēlia advēnit ad tabernam mercātōris, _____ glīrēs optimōs vēndēbat.   _____

6. Which woman wants to buy dormice?

_____ fēmina glīrēs emere vult?   _____

7. The woman, who wants to buy dormice, is Aurelia.

Fēmina, _____ glīrēs emere vult, est Aurēlia.   _____

8. A slave, whom Cornelia saw, was carrying a pig.

Servus, _____ Cornēlia vīdit, porcum portābat.   _____

9. A certain man was angry because he could not avoid the pig.

Vir _____ īrātus erat _____ porcum vītāre nōn paterat.   _____

                    _____

Forms

Indefinite Adjectives

Activity 29f The Indefinite Adjective *quīdam, quaedam, quoddam*

Fill in the spaces with the correct form of the indefinite adjective to agree with the underlined noun. When you are finished, copy the circled letters in order below, and you will find a form of the indefinite adjective.

1. Aurēlia petit <u>tabernam</u> ◯ ___ ___ ___ ___ ___ ___, quae nōn procul abest.

2. Pecūniam <u>mercātōrī</u> ___ ◯ ___ ___ ___ ___ dabit.

3. Aurēlia glīrēs ā <u>mercātōre</u> ___ ___ ◯ ___ ___ ___ emere solet.

4. Glīrēs <u>mercātōrum</u> ___ ___ ◯ ___ ___ ___ nōn bonī sunt.

5. Necesse est igitur ad <u>mercātōrem</u> ___ ◯ ___ ___ ___ ___ īre.

6. Tabernae <u>mercātōrum</u> ___ ___ ___ ◯ ___ ___ sordidae sunt.

7. Hodiē Aurēlia per <u>viās</u> ___ ___ ___ ___ ◯ ___ celeriter ībat.

8. <u>Amīcae</u> ___ ___ ◯ ___ ___ ___ eī optimōs mercātōrēs dēmōnstrāvērunt.

9. <u>Senātōrēs</u> ___ ___ ___ ___ ___ ◯, quōs Cornēlius ad cēnam invītāvit, laetī erunt.

___ ___ ___ ___ ___ . ___ ___ ___

Interrogative Pronouns

Activity 29g Who or What?

Match the Latin questions here and on page 13 to the correct answers:

1. Quī sunt parentēs Mārcī et Cornēliae? _____   **a.** Phrygia.

2. Quis est ancilla Aurēliae? _____   **b.** Cornēliī.

3. Quid mendīcī petēbant? _____   **c.** Aurēlia et Cornēlius.

4. Cuius frāter est Titus? _____   **d.** Mercātōrī.

5. Cui dabit pecūniam Aurēlia?   _____   e. Hominem obēsum.

6. Quācum Aurēlia in urbem ībat?   _____   f. Mārcī.

7. Quid recitābant poētae?   _____   g. Cum Cornēliā.

8. Quī sunt līberī Aurēliae?   _____   h. Pecūniam.

9. Quem in lectīcā Cornēlia vīdit?   _____   i. Versūs.

10. Cuius soror est Cornēlia?   _____   j. Mārcus et Cornēlia.

Applying What You Have Learned

Activity 29h Writing the Language

Translate the following English sentences into Latin. Include all long marks. Use the story and vocabulary lists in your textbook, as well as the vocabulary lists in this book, to help you:

1. What delighted you in the city today, my daughter?

   _____

2. The litter, in which the freedman was reclining, was most elegant.

   _____

3. How fast that pig was running through the crowd!

   _____

4. A certain man, who had fallen into the mud, was exceedingly angry.

   _____

5. We did not, however, see the end of the quarrel because our slaves carried us into another street.

   _____

Activity 29i Expanding Your English Vocabulary

For each italicized English word below, give the related Latin word and below it the meaning of that Latin word. Then complete each sentence by filling in a word at the right:

Latin Word
Meaning of the Latin Word   **If you …**

1. _____   give money to a *mendicant*
   _____   on the street, you give it to a   _____

2. _____   eat in a *recumbent* position,
   _____   you eat while you are   _____

3. _____   take a *final* exam, you take
                                    an exam that marks the
   _____   _____ of the school year.   _____

4. _____   give a slave *liberty*, you give
                                    him his
   _____   _____

5. _____   enjoy a *delectable* meal, you
                                    are _____ by the food.
   _____   _____

6. _____   are *fuming* with anger, you are
                                    (figuratively speaking) "hot"
   _____   enough to produce   _____

7. _____   wear royal *vestments*, you
                                    wear the _____ of a king.
   _____   _____

8. _____   *rupture* a dam, you cause
                                    it to
   _____   _____

9. _____   travel on a *mesa*, you travel on a
                                    flat plateau, the name of which is
   _____   a Spanish word derived from the
                                    Latin word for   _____

10. _____   *fumigate* the attic, you fill the attic
                                    with _____ containing pesticides
   _____   to drive out vermin or insects.   _____

Activity 29j Reading Latin

Look at the new vocabulary beneath this story. Then read the story, noting the interrogative pronouns and adjectives and the indefinite adjectives. Reread the story for comprehension. Then answer the questions that follow with complete Latin sentences.

What's Going on Here?

Mārcus, quī in peristyliō sedēbat et legēbat, subitō audīvit fragōrem.

Mārcus: Quem in tablīnō patris audīvī? Quis es? Esne servus? Quam ob causam in tablīnō es?

Sextus: *(quī in peristylium rumpit)* Salvē, Mārce! Mē cēlābam quod Eucleidēs mē petēbat. Ēheu! Librī quīdam patris tuī in solum cecidērunt! *(Puerī ad ātrium appropinquant.)* Quam occupātī sunt servī! Cūr hūc illūc festīnant? Quid accidit?

Mārcus: Servī strēnuē labōrant quod pater meus complūrēs ad cēnam invītāvit. Cēnam ēlegantissimam et ingentem parābit coquus noster. Hodiē igitur servī et ancillae domum pūrgant.

Sextus: Quōs invītāvit pater tuus?

Mārcus: Invītāvit pater senātōrēs quōsdam et clientēs, quī ab omnibus partibus urbis ad domum nostram venient.

Sextus: Quōs senātōrēs ad hanc cēnam invītāvit? Quī convīvae hīc cēnābunt?

Mārcus: Senātōrēs quī sunt amīcī eius invītāvit. Etiam apud nōs cēnābunt senātōrēs quī patrem meum ad cēnam invītāvērunt. Certē Titus, patruus meus, quoque aderit. Quōrum vōcēs audīmus?

Sextus: Audīmus vōcēs ancillārum quārundam quae trīclīnium et ātrium pūrgant.

Mārcus: Mox afferent ad trīclīnium candēlābra et ōrnāmenta et lectōs, in quibus convīvae recumbere solent dum cēnant.

Sextus: Quibuscum illā nocte cēnābimus ego et tū? Cum senātōribus, cum clientibus? Ego sum fīlius senātōris praeclārī!

Mārcus: *(cum rīsū)* Ēheu! Cum Cornēliā cēnābimus, nam puerī sumus, nōn senātōrēs.

solum, -ī, n., *floor*

complūrēs, -ēs, -a, *several, many*

coquus, -ī, m., *cook*

candēlābrum, -ī, n., *candelabrum, lamp-stand*

ōrnāmenta, -ōrum, n., *furnishings*

convīva, -ae, m., *guest (at a banquet)*

1. Quem in tablīnō audīvit Mārcus?

_____

2. Ā quō fugit Sextus?

_____

3. Quibuscum Cornēlius cēnābit?

_____

4. Cuius amicōs invītāvit Cornēlius?

_____

5. Quem quoque invītāvit Cornēlius?

_____

6. In quibus convīvae recumbunt dum cēnant?

_____

7. Quid ad trīclīnium portābunt servī quīdam?

_____

FIRE!

> *In addition to vocabulary and the story, the activities for this chapter focus on:*
> 1. passive forms of verbs in the present, imperfect, and future tenses.
> 2. passive forms of the irregular verb **ferō**.
> 3. transformation of verbs from active to passive.

Vocabulary

Activity 30a Vocabulary

Study the vocabulary list on page 197 alone or with a partner.

The Story

Activity 30b Vocabulary in Context

Fill in the blanks to match the English cues:

1. Aurēlia cōnspexit _____, ē quā magna _____

   flammārum _____ fūmī ēmittēbātur. (apartment building)
   (force/amount) (and)

2. Adstantēs _____ servāre nōn possunt. (tenants)

3. Nōs omnēs _____ mox _____. (by fire) (will be
   overwhelmed)

4. Mātrēs ā līberīs _____ _____. (small) (were being sought)

5. Ab illīs mulieribus miserīs _____. (I am moved/upset)

6. Cista ē _____ _____. (the window) (is thrown out)

7. _____ _____ ā mātribus vestrīs

   _____. (without doubt) (you will be saved)

8. Flammae ad vōs _____ advēnerant. (almost)

9. Spectāculum _____ miserābile numquam anteā vīdī. (so)

Forms

Passive Verbs: Present, Imperfect, and Future

Activity 30c Matching Passive Verbs with Their Meanings

Match the verbs at the left with meanings at the right. Note that the passive of the verb **vidēre** *often means* to seem. *There are more meanings than you will need:*

Verbs

1. vidētur _____
2. audiēbāmur _____
3. audiēminī _____
4. audiēbāris _____
5. videor _____
6. vidēbimur _____
7. vidēbuntur _____
8. audītur _____
9. audiēris _____
10. audīris _____
11. videntur _____
12. audiuntur _____
13. vidēbor _____
14. vidēminī _____
15. audīminī _____

Meanings

a. we will be seen / we will seem

b. it is heard

c. they are being seen / they seem

d. she is seen / she seems

e. she will be seen / she will seem

f. you (sing.) will be heard

g. you (pl.) will be heard

h. I will be seen / I will seem

i. you (sing.) are being heard

j. I will be heard

k. you (pl.) are heard

l. I am seen / I seem

m. he will be heard

n. they are heard

o. we were being heard

p. they will be seen / they will seem

q. you (pl.) are being seen / you seem

r. you (sing.) were being heard

s. we were seen / we seemed

Activity 30d Passive Forms

For each verb, give its infinitive and conjugation number (or irreg.) at the left and then fill in the missing passive forms:

Infinitive	Conj.	Present	Imperfect	Future
1. _____	_____	_____	pōnēbātur	_____
2. _____	_____	spectāmur	_____	_____
3. _____	_____	_____	_____	cōnspicientur
4. _____	_____	vidēris	_____	_____
5. _____	_____	quaeror	_____	_____
6. _____	_____	_____	_____	rogābitur
7. _____	_____	_____	petēbāminī	_____
8. _____	_____	_____	_____	tenēbitur
9. _____	_____	opprimur	_____	_____
10. _____	_____	_____	servābar	_____
11. _____	_____	_____	_____	ferēris
12. _____	_____	_____	audiēbāminī	_____

Activity 30e Transforming Verbs from Active to Passive

Change each of the following verbs from active to passive voice, keeping the same person and number; then translate both verbs. The first one is done for you:

1. trahēbam   *I was dragging*

   trahēbar   *I was being dragged*

2. agit   _____

   _____   _____

3. mittis   _____

   _____   _____

4. tenēbis   _____

   _____   _____

5. servātis

_____

_____

6. commovēs

_____

_____

7. relinquam

_____

_____

8. exspectābātis

_____

_____

9. cūrāmus

_____

_____

10. audiēs

_____

_____

11. vidēbō

_____

_____

12. audit

_____

_____

The Irregular Verb *ferō*

Activity 30f Passive Forms of *ferō*

Fill in the blanks to match the English cues:

1. Nōnnumquam ad Cūriam senātōrēs _____. (are carried)

2. Cornēlius, "Ego ad Forum heri nōn _____," inquit. (was being carried)

3. Eucleidēs, "Ego numquam ad Argīlētum _____," inquit. (will be carried)

4. "_____ celeriter ad tabernam, Cornēlia?" (Were you being carried?)

5. "Ita vērō, nōs eō summā celeritāte _____." (were being carried)

6. "_____ eō crās, Aurēlia?" (Will you be carried?)

7. "Ego et Cornēlia eō _____." (will be carried)

8. Aqua ad aedificium ab adstantibus _____. (is being carried)

9. Vōs ex aedificiō ab adstantibus _____. (are being carried)

10. Ā mātre nōn _____ nisi parvula es. (are carried)

Applying What You Have Learned

Activity 30g Writing the Language

Translate the following English sentences into Latin. Include all long marks. Use the story and vocabulary lists in your textbook, as well as the vocabulary lists in this book, to help you. Use the imperfect for all past tenses:

1. The apartment building was almost hidden by smoke and flames.

   _____

2. All the bystanders are upset by the miserable sight.

   _____

   _____

3. Little children, who were being held by their mothers, were weeping.

   _____

4. Will the children be found by their own parents in this huge crowd?

   _____

5. Help will not be brought to those poor tenants. They will not be saved.

   _____

Activity 30h Expanding Your English Vocabulary

Using the word bank below, write the word that could replace the italicized word or words in each sentence. Use the Latin words in parentheses to help determine the meaning of the English words. Then write the English translation of each Latin word in the word bank:

1. Aurelia tried to *separate* Cornelia from the dangers of the city, as if she were placing her on an island away from harm. _____

2. Oil lamps used in Roman houses were *fire-causing* hazards. _____

3. Cornelia wondered what all the *disturbance* was about. _____

4. Italy's land mass is *almost an island*. _____

5. The apartment building was *sending out* smoke and flames. _____

6. Aurelia was reluctant to answer Cornelia's *question* about the victims of the fire. _____

7. The Romans rejected monarchy because some kings had tried to *overwhelm* the people. _____

8. The intruders were being *thrown out* from the courtroom. _____

9. Parents were running around in a frantic *search* for their children. _____

10. The fate of that woman and her children is *uncertain*. _____

quest (**quaerere**) _____	incendiary (**incendium**) _____
emitting (**ēmittere**) _____	dubious (**dubium**) _____
oppress (**opprimere**) _____	commotion (**commovēre**) _____
insulate (**īnsula**) _____	ejected (**ēicere**) _____
peninsula (**paene + īnsula**)	query (**quaerere**) _____
_____ + _____	

Activity 30i Reading Latin

Look at the new vocabulary beneath this story. Then read the story, noting the passive verb forms. Reread the Latin for comprehension. Then correct the statements following the story by completing the sentences properly:

Sights and Surprises in the City

Cornēlius est vir honestissimus, quem multī laudant. Uxor eius quoque ā cīvibus laudātur. Cornēlius et Aurēlia ab amīcīs ad cēnam saepe invītantur. Cornēlius, quī amīcōs quōsdam ad cēnam invītāre solet, heri ad cēnam complūrēs amīcōs invītāvit. Aurēlia igitur et Cornēlia glīrēs in forō heri ēmērunt.

Aurēlia, quamquam multās pulchrāsque vestēs habet, saepe tamen novās vestēs emit. Hodiē, quod Cornēlius ad cēnam amīcōs invītāvit, stolam novam emere vult. Eī igitur necesse est in urbem iterum dēscendere. Cornēlia quoque cum mātre in urbem ībit, nam puellae Rōmānae ā mātre sīc ēducantur. Hodiē Cornēlia māterque in urbem sellīs ferentur.

Stat in viā prope aedificium quoddam ingēns plaustrum, in quō sunt ingentēs lapidēs. Hoc plaustrum ab omnibus vītātur quod nōnnumquam lapidēs ex eō cadunt et adstantēs necantur. Līberī saepissimē dē tālibus viārum perīculīs ā Cornēliō monentur. Hodiē lectīcāriī per viās angustās vix prōcēdere possunt quod ab adstantibus impediuntur.

Aurēlia et Cornēlia, dum per viās hominum plēnās prōcēdunt, Sextō forte occurrunt. Ille ab Aurēliā īrā commōtā reprehenditur, "Quid hīc agis, Sexte? Nōnne pater Mārcī tē vetuit sōlum ē domō exīre? Tibi nōn licet in urbem sine custōde excēdere. Domī esse dēbēs. Sine dubiō ā Cornēliō īrātō pūniēris."

Subitō magnus clāmor in viīs audītur. Procul vident iterum īnsulam quandam, cuius ē fenestrīs ēmittuntur flammae et fūmus. Clāmōrēs incolārum miserōrum audiuntur. Concursant multī hominēs hūc illūc. Ōrnāmenta ab incolīs ē fenestrīs ēiciuntur. Statim aqua ad īnsulam ā multīs hominibus portātur. Dum incendium Aurēlia et Cornēlia spectant, aufugit Sextus. Prīmum mediā turbā sē cēlat, deinde summā celeritāte domum redit.

> **honestissimus, -a, -um,** *highly respected, most distinguished*
>
> **complūrēs, -ēs, -a,** *several*
>
> **-que,** enclitic conjunction, *and*
>
> **sīc,** adv., *thus, in this way*
>
> **ēducō, -āre,** *to educate, raise*
>
> **saepissimē,** adv., *very often*
>
> **moneō, monēre, monuī, monitus,** *to warn*
>
> **angustus, -a, -um,** *narrow*

prōcēdō, prōcēdere, prōcessī, prōcessūrus, *to go forward, proceed*

excēdō, excēdere, excessī, excessūrus, *to go out*

1. Cornēlius, vir honestissimus, ā multīs vītātur.

   Cornēlius, vir honestissimus, _____

2. Stola nova ab Aurēliā laudābitur.

   Stola nova _____

3. Servī Cornēliam Aurēliamque in urbem ēicient.

   Servī Cornēliam Aurēliamque _____

4. Adstantēs lectīcāriōs, quī per viās angustās vix cadēbant, obscūrābant.

   Adstantēs lectīcāriōs, _____

5. Sextus ā Cornēliō ē domō sōlus exīre parātur.

   Sextus _____

6. Incolae ōrnāmenta ē fenestrīs vident.

   Incolae ōrnāmenta _____

7. Sextus, dum aufugit, turbā opprimitur.

   Sextus, dum aufugit, _____

PSEUDOLUS

Go Online
PHSchool.com
Web Code: jgd-0004

In addition to vocabulary and the story, the activities in this chapter focus on:

1. present passive infinitives.
2. the uses of the ablative case to express time, manner, means, cause, and price and the use of the ablative case with passive verbs.
3. the demonstrative adjectives and pronouns **ipse, ipsa, ipsum** and **īdem, eadem, idem.**

Vocabulary

Activity 31a Vocabulary

Study the vocabulary list on pages 198–199 alone or with a partner.

The Story

Activity 31b Questions on the Story

Answer the following questions with full sentences in Latin. Use your book and base your answers on the story at the beginning of Chapter 31.

1. Quid audītur ab eīs quī per ātrium ambulant?

_____

2. Quid Pseudolus lanium rogāvit?

_____

3. Dabitne Pseudolus tantum pretium?

_____

4. Habetne alius lanius in hāc viā meliōrem carnem?

_____

5. Sī Pseudolus multum emet, quid accidet?

_____

6. Ā quō porcus cūrābātur?

_____

7. Cui lanius porcum vēndere vult?

_____

8. Quī rēctē praedōnēs vocantur?

_____

9. Quot dēnāriīs porcus et lepus Pseudolō trāduntur?

_____

10. Quid Aurēlia in animō habet facere?

_____

Forms

Present Passive Infinitives

Activity 31c Transforming Infinitives from Active to Passive

Fill in the blanks in the paragraph below, and then change each of the following present active infinitives to passive:

In the 1st, 2nd, and 4th conjugations, the present passive infinitive is made by dropping the final _____ from the active infinitive and adding the letter _____. In the 3rd conjugation, the present passive infinitive is made by dropping the letters _____ from the active infinitive and adding the letter _____.

1. iubēre _____

2. pūnīre _____

3. trādere _____

4. revocāre _____

Activity 31d Passive Infinitives

The verb in each of the following sentences needs an infinitive to complete its meaning. Fill in the blank with the passive form of the infinitive from the accompanying word bank that makes the best sense according to the stories you have read so far. (Not all infinitives will be used.) Then translate the sentences:

1. Cornēlius raedam ē fossā _____ iussit.

_____

2. Aurēlia porcum pinguem _____ volēbat.

_____

3. Porcus ā laniō _____ nōlēbat.

_____

4. Aurēlia Pseudolum _____ vult.

_____

5. Pseudolus in urbe _____ volēbat.

_____

| pūnīre | emere | mittere | extrahere | capere | iacere | retinēre |

Building the Meaning

The Ablative Case (Consolidation)

Activity 31e Uses of the Ablative Case

In each sentence, circle the ablative(s) or ablative phrase(s) that match one of the categories below. Identify how the ablatives are used by writing the number of the appropriate category on the line at the right. Then translate the sentences:

1. Time when   **5. Cause**

2. Time within which   **6. Price**

3. Instrument or means   **7. Personal agent with passive verb**

4. Manner

1. Pōrcī in agrīs aestāte manent.   _____

_____

2. Heri porcus quīdam pinguis manū laniī ipsīus pascēbātur.   _____

_____

_____

3. Hodiē lanius Pseudolō eundem porcum magnō pretiō vēndere vult.   ————

_____

_____

4. Lepus quoque additur grātīs. Ille porcus et hic lepus mox ā servō   ————
procācī per viās feruntur.

_____

_____

5. Pseudolus optimō iocō cēterōs servōs dēlectāre potest.   ————

_____

_____

6. Iocus ā Syrō in culīnā nārrātur.   ————

_____

7. Pseudolus tamen ā dominā reprehenditur.   ————

_____

8. Brevī tempore ad vīllam rūsticam mittētur.   ————

_____

9. Pseudolus magnā cum īrā cēterīs servīs clāmat, "Vestrā culpā ego   ————
puniar, quod cachinnus vester maximus erat."   ————

_____

_____

Forms

Demonstrative Adjectives and Pronouns

Activity 31f Comparison of Forms

*Fill in the blanks to match the English cues. In each set, put the adjectives **ille, hic,** and **īdem** before the nouns they modify and the adjective **ipse** after the noun it modifies:*

1. Mercātor leporem vēndit.

_____ _____ leporem vēndit. (That merchant)

_____ _____ leporem vēndit. (This merchant)

_____ _____ leporem alium vēndidit.
(The same merchant)

_____ _____ leporem vēndidit. (The merchant himself)

2. Pseudolus laniō pecūniam trādit.

Pseudolus _____ _____ pecūniam trādit. (to that butcher)

Pseudolus _____ _____ pecūniam trādit. (to this butcher)

Alius servus _____ _____ pecūniam trādidit. (to the same butcher)

Pseudolus _____ _____ pecūniam trādidit. (to the butcher himself)

3. Īra dominae erat magna.

Īra _____ _____ erat magna. (of that mistress)

Īra _____ _____ erat magna. (of this mistress)

Īra _____ _____ erat magna. (of the same mistress)

Īra _____ _____ erat magna. (of the mistress herself)

4. Pretium leporum erat octō dēnāriī.

Pretium _____ _____ erat octō dēnāriī. (of those hares)

Pretium _____ _____ erat octō dēnāriī. (of these hares)

Pretium _____ _____ erat octō dēnāriī. (of the same hares)

Pretium _____ _____ erat octō dēnāriī. (of the hares themselves)

5. Numquam Messalla ad cēnam sine clientibus venit.

Numquam Messalla ad cēnam sine _____ _____ venit. (those clients)

Numquam Messalla ad cēnam sine _____ _____ venit. (these clients)

Numquam Messalla ad cēnam sine _____ _____ venit. (the same clients)

Numquam Messalla ad cēnam sine _____ _____ venit. (the clients themselves)

Applying What You Have Learned

Activity 31g Writing the Language

Translate the following English sentences into Latin. Include all long marks. Use the stories and vocabulary lists in your textbook, as well as the vocabulary lists in this book, to help you:

1. Loud laughter was heard by Marcus and Sextus.

_____

2. That merchant ordered this hare to be added gratis.

_____

3. The pig itself was being led through the door into the kitchen.

_____

4. Cornelius himself will never order Pseudolus to be sent to the country house and farm.

_____

5. Cornelius never invites the same guests to dinner.

_____

Activity 31h Expanding Your English Vocabulary

For each italicized English word below, give the related Latin word and below it the meaning of that Latin word. Then complete each sentence by filling in a word at the right:

Latin Word
Meaning of the Latin Word   **If you ...**

1. _____   *diminish* the amount of homework
   _____   you have to do, you _____ it.   _____

2. _____   use gasoline that has *additives* in
   _____   it, you use gasoline to which
                                 various substances have been   _____

3. _____   *reprehend* someone for bad behavior,
   _____   you _____ the person.   _____

4. _____   wish to buy a *precious* stone, you
   _____   will have to pay a high _____ for it.   _____

5. _____   *accept* a gift, you _____ it.
   _____   _____

6. _____   are behaving *correctly*, you are
   _____   acting in a _____ manner.   _____

7. _____   have a *carnivore* as a pet, your
   _____   pet feeds on   _____

8. _____   are considered a *celebrity*,
   _____   you must be a _____ person.   _____

9. _____   try to *rectify* a situation, you
   _____   try to make it   _____

10. _____   are in a *pasture*, you are in a place
    _____   where animals _____ on the grass.   _____

Activity 31i Reading Latin

Look at the new vocabulary following this story. Then read the Latin of the story, noting passive infinitives, ablatives, and demonstrative adjectives and pronouns. Reread the Latin for comprehension. Then match the first part of each sentence that follows to the phrase or clause that correctly completes it:

Always an Answer

Īrāta adhūc erat Aurēlia quod Pseudolus, ille servus procāx, leporem comparāverat. Itaque ad culīnam iit. Vexāta, "Servī scelestī," inquit, "vōs nōn iussī leporem emere."

Coquus metū commōtus, "Cūr nōs omnēs reprehendis, mea domina? Pseudolus enim, ille servus scelestus, sōlus leporem ēmit."

Aurēlia cōnspexit Pseudolum illum procācem, quī eī appropinquābat. "Dīc mihi," inquit domina īrāta, "cūr tū illum leporem ēmistī?"

Cui servus, "At nōn ēmī, domina. Lanius, ut bene scīs, praedō est. Ille magnō pretiō porcum vēndere volēbat. Ego tantum pretium eī dare nōlēbam, sed melior porcus eōdem pretiō invenīrī nōn potuit. Prīmō ille lanius pretium minuere nōluit, sed tandem dēfessus victōriam mihi concessit. Invītus leporem mihi grātīs dedit. Quid facerem? Leporem domum tulī."

Cui Aurēlia, "Servīs dōna accipere nōn licet. Illum leporem in Forō vēnīre iubēbō."

At procāciter respondit Pseudolus, "Cūr leporem mihi adimere vīs? Nōnne mihi quoque licet bonam cēnam habēre?"

"Puer procāx et scelestus es! Nōn sine causā tū Pseudolus ā servīs vocāris! Tū quoque es praedō. Leporem propter avāritiam tuam comparāvistī. Dominus tuus tē hīc manēre nōn sinet. Sine dubiō paucīs diēbus ad vīllam tē mittet neque hūc redīre sinet." Tum Aurēlia ē culīnā īrāta exit.

Deinde ūnus ē servīs, "Pseudole," inquit, "tē saepe dē īrā dominae prius monuimus, sed frūstrā. Nōs omnēs hodiē īrā dominae vexāmur, at tū diū dolēbis, cum in agrīs labōrābis."

Sed Pseudolus cum rīsū, "Immō errātis neque rēctē dīcitis, amīcī meī. Ego neque senātōrēs neque vīlicōs timeō. Ego certē semper laetus, semper sēcūrus sum. In illō locō fortasse leporēs capiam et laniō cuidam vēndam."

comparō, -āre, -āvī, -ātus, *to buy*
coquus, -ī, m., *cook*
prīmō, adv., *at first*
concēdō, concēdere, concessī, concessus, *to yield, give up, grant*
Quid facerem? *What was I to do?*
dōnum, -ī, n., *gift*
vēneō, vēnīre, vēniī, *to go for sale, to be sold*

adimō, adimere, adēmī, adēmptus + dat., *to take away (from)*
avāritia, -ae, f., *greed*
sinō, sinere, sīvī, situs, *to allow*
hūc, adv., *to this place, here*
moneō, -ēre, -uī, -itus, *to advise, warn*
sēcūrus, -a, -um, *carefree, unconcerned*

1. Aurēlia culīnam intrāvit et īrāta fuit quod . . . _____

2. Coquus Aurēliam timēbat quod . . . _____

3. Quod Pseudolus magnum pretium laniō dare nōlēbat . . . _____

4. Aurēlia leporem Pseudolō darī nōlēbat quod . . . _____

5. Paucīs diēbus Pseudolus in agrīs labōrābit quod . . . _____

6. Aurelia īrā commōta vexābat aliōs servōs quī . . . _____

7. Pseudolus sēcūrus tandem erat quod . . . _____

a. . . . prope vīllam leporēs capī et vēnīre potuērunt.

b. . . . Pseudolum dē īrā eius prius monuerant.

c. . . . ā dominā reprehendī nōluit.

d. . . . Cornēlius eum ad vīllam propter avāritiam eius mittet.

e. . . . leporem grātīs eī dedit lanius.

f. . . . leporem emī nōn iussit.

g. . . . servīs Cornēliī dōna accipere nōn licēbat.

DINNER PREPARATIONS

Go Online
PHSchool.com
Web Code: jgd-0005

In addition to vocabulary and the story, the activities for this chapter focus on:
1. passive forms of verbs in the perfect, pluperfect, and future perfect tenses.
2. transformation of verbs from active to passive and vice versa.
3. agreement of perfect passive verbs with their subjects.

Vocabulary

Activity 32a Vocabulary

Study the vocabulary list on pages 200–201 alone or with a partner.

The Story

Activity 32b Questions on the Story — Who Did What?

The story in Chapter 32 describes a busy time for the household of the Cornelii. Without looking in your textbook, complete the answers to the following questions:

1. Ā quō amīci invītātī erant?   _____ amīcī invītātī erant.

2. Ā quō glīrēs ēmptī erant?   _____ glīrēs ēmptī erant.

3. Ā quibus pānis compārātus est?   _____ pānis compārātus est.

4. Ā quibus multus cibus coctus est?   _____ multus cibus coctus
                                                   est.

5. Ā quibus lectī in trīclīniō positī sunt?   _____ lectī in trīclīniō
                                                   positī sunt.

6. Ā quō mortuī ad Charōnem addūcēbantur?   _____ mortuī ad Charōnem
                                                   addūcēbantur.

7. Ā quō ancillae incitābantur?   _____ ancillae incitābantur.

8. Ā quō candēlābrum ēversum est?   _____ candēlābrum
                                                   ēversum est.

9. Ā quō ignis exstīnctus est?   _____ ignis exstīnctus est.

10. Ā quibus alia strāta lāta sunt?   _____ et

                                                   _____ alia strāta lāta sunt.

11. Ā quibus mappae ferēbantur? _____ mappae ferēbantur.

12. Ā quō convīvae salūtātī sunt? _____ convīvae salūtātī sunt.

13. Quis paulisper exspectātus est? _____ paulisper exspectātus est.

14. Ā quibus soleae ablātae sunt? _____ soleae ablātae sunt.

Forms

Verbs: Perfect, Pluperfect, and Future Perfect Passive

Activity 32c Passive Forms

Give the perfect, pluperfect, and future perfect passive forms of the verbs listed in the first column in the person, number, and gender requested. The first set is done for you:

1st Principal Part	Person, Number, Gender	Perfect Passive	Pluperfect Passive	Future Perfect Passive
videō	1st sing. m.	*vīsus sum*	*vīsus eram*	*vīsus erō*
1. coquō	3rd sing. n.	_____	_____	_____
2. ēvertere	3rd pl. n.	_____	_____	_____
3. invītāre	1st sing. m.	_____	_____	_____
4. iubēre	1st pl. m.	_____	_____	_____
5. addūcere	2nd sing. f.	_____	_____	_____
6. effundō	2nd pl. m.	_____	_____	_____
7. afferre	3rd. pl. f.	_____	_____	_____
8. dēiciō	1st. pl. f.	_____	_____	_____
9. salūtāre	2nd sing. m.	_____	_____	_____
10. auferre	3rd sing. n.	_____	_____	_____

Activity 32d Matching Passive Verbs with Meanings

Match the verbs at the left with meanings at the right. There are more meanings than you will need:

Verbs

Meanings

1. vīsī erāmus _____

a. we will have been seen

2. audītum erat _____

b. it will have been seen

3. audītae estis _____

c. you will have been heard (pl.)

4. audīta sunt _____

d. she was seen

5. vīsum erit _____

e. we had been seen

6. vīsae erātis _____

f. I was seen

7. vīsī sumus _____

g. you were heard (pl.)

8. audītus es _____

h. he will have been seen

9. audīta erō _____

i. it had been heard

10. audītae erimus _____

j. you have been heard (sing.)

11. vīsus es _____

k. you had been seen (pl.)

12. audītī eritis _____

l. I will have been heard

13. vīsa sum _____

m. he will have been heard

14. vīsī erunt _____

n. he was heard

15. audītus est _____

o. those things were heard

p. you were seen (sing.)

q. they will have been seen

r. we will have been heard

s. we were seen

Name _____ Date _____ Period _____

Activity 32e Transformations

Change each of the following verbs from active to passive voice, keeping the same tense, person, and number; then translate both verbs. The gender of the implied subject of each verb is indicated in parentheses. Use this information to determine the ending of the perfect passive participle. The first set is done for you:

1. iussit (masc. subject)   *he ordered/has ordered* _____

     iussus est _____   *he was ordered/has been ordered* _____

2. audīverat (fem. subject)   _____

_____   _____

3. trāxistī (fem. subject)   _____

_____   _____

4. parāvimus (masc. subject)   _____

_____   _____

5. mīserō (fem. subject)   _____

_____   _____

6. commōverant (masc. subject) _____

_____   _____

7. portāveritis (masc. subject)   _____

_____   _____

8. attulerāmus (fem. subject)   _____

_____   _____

9. oppressit (neut. subject)   _____

_____   _____

10. ēiēcī (masc. subject)   _____

_____   _____

Activity 32f **Tranformations in Context**

Rewrite the following sentences using passive forms of the verbs and making other changes as necessary. The first one is done for you.

1. Cornēlius illōs amīcōs ad cēnam invītāverat.

   Illī amīcī ā Cornēliō ad cēnam invītātī erant.

2. Aurēlia fīliae, "Herī," inquit, "ego tē in urbem dūxī."

   _____

3. Crās tertiā hōrā ego glīrēs emam.

   _____

4. Pseudolus porcum tulit.

   _____

5. "Domina mē," inquit Pseudolus, "ad tabernam laniī mīsit."

   _____

6. Aurēlia servōs in Forum mīserat.

   _____

7. Servī ōva et māla comparāvērunt.

   _____

8. Clāmōrēs incolārum miserōrum Cornēliam terruerant.

   _____

9. "Aurēlia et Cornēlia, "Illa māter et illī līberī," inquiunt, "nōs valdē commōvērunt."

   _____

10. Flammae et fūmus magnum aedificium oppressērunt.

   _____

Applying What You Have Learned

Activity 32g Writing the Language

Translate the following English sentences into Latin. Include all long marks. Use the stories and vocabulary lists in your textbook, as well as the vocabulary lists in this book, to help you:

1. After the food was bought, Syra and Phrygia were called to the kitchen by Aurelia.

    _____

2. Because several distinguished guests had been invited, it was necessary to prepare a very good dinner.

    _____

3. Why was Cerberus dragged out of the underworld? Hercules had been ordered to bring that dog to the light.

    _____

4. The fire has been put out by the senator, and the frightened slave-woman will no longer be scolded.

    _____

5. When all the food is/will have been cooked, it will be brought into the dining room.

    _____

Activity 32h Word Study

Using the word bank below, write the word that could replace the italicized word or words in each sentence. Use the Latin words in parentheses to help determine the meaning of the English words. Then write the English translation of each Latin word in the word bank:

1. When the lamp fell, it *set fire to* the sheet.   _____

2. Because of the quick action of Cornelius, there were no *victims* from the fire.   _____

3. The food will be brought in on large, *egg-shaped* trays.   _____

4. After being scolded by Aurelia, the slave was *in low spirits*.   _____

5. The emperor *rules* with the power of a king.   _____

6. Pseudolus tried to *go around* the instructions he had been given.   _____

7. Eucleides was *gushing* in his praise of the city's buildings. _____

8. Meeting Cornelius in the Forum was a *chance* event. _____

9. Volcanic activity has provided Italy with many deposits of
fire-born rock. _____

10. Eucleides used *a roundabout way of talking* to describe the more _____
sordid areas of the city.

circumvent (**circum**) _____	ignited (**ignis**) _____
oval (**ōvum**) _____	dejected (**dēicere**) _____
effusive (**effundere**) _____	circumlocution (**circum**) _____
igneous (**ignis**) _____	casual (**cāsū**) _____ ,
casualties (**cāsū**) _____ ,	
	reigns (**rēgnum**) _____

Activity 32i Reading Latin

*Look at the new vocabulary following this story. Then read the Latin of the story, noting verbs
in the perfect, pluperfect, and future perfect passive. Reread the Latin for comprehension.
Then complete the statements about the story with the correct information:*

Tell Me about This Hero!

Cornēlius, postquam in trīclīnium intrāvit, Cornēliam vīdit. Cornēlia

pictūram, quae in pariete erat, spectābat. "Quid tū facis, mea fīlia?" inquit

Cornēlius.

Cui Cornēlia, "Haec pictūra pulcherrima mihi placet, pater. Nōnne hic vir

est Herculēs? Multa dē Hercule nōbīs ab Eucleide nārrāta sunt, sed ego omnia

audīre volō."

Respondit Cornēlius, "Herculēs, ut bene scīs, erat vir Graecus. Ōlim ubi

īnfāns erat, in lectō dormiēbat. Subitō duo serpentēs lectō appropinquāvērunt et Herculem necāre temptāvērunt. Herculēs autem, quamquam parvulus erat, ē

somnō excitātus, serpentēs sōlus manibus strangulāvit."

Cornēlia tamen rogāvit, "Sed cūr in pictūrā est canis trifōrmis? Cūr hic

canis ab Hercule trahitur?"

Eī respondit pater, "Herculēs, quod dēmēns fīliōs suōs ōlim necāverat, trīstis

erat et sē pūnīre cōnstituit. Itaque factus est servus rēgis cuiusdam superbī, quī

tamen eum valdē timēbat. Herculēs ā rēge multōs labōrēs perficere iussus est. Ille

canis, quem in pictūrā vidēs, est Cerberus, quī portās īnferōrum custōdit. In hāc

pictūrā Cerberum invītum Herculēs ex īnferīs trahit. Ā rēge enim Herculēs in

rēgnum īnfernum dēscendere iussus erat, quod rēx sēcum ita cōgitābat: "Herculēs

numquam ex īnferīs redībit. Sine dubiō ā Cerberō necābitur." Sed tandem ex

īnferīs Herculēs exit cum cane. Itaque rēx perterritus Herculem iussit canem ad

īnferōs statim redūcere."

At iam vōx Aurēliae ā patre et fīliā audīta est. "Ēheu!" clāmāvit Cornēlia.

"Māter nōs vocat. Īrāta esse solet sī sērō venīmus. Mox erit cēnae tempus. Nōnne

senātōrēs quīdam apud nōs hodiē cēnābunt?"

"Ita vērō!" respondit Cornēlius, "crās tamen dē aliīs Herculis labōribus tibi

multa nārrābō."

Herculēs, Herculis, m., *Hercules*	**rēx, rēgis,** m., *king*
trifōrmis, -is, -e, *three-headed*	**superbus, -a, -um,** *proud, arrogant*
dēmēns, dēmentis, *out of one's mind, mad*	**perficiō, perficere, perfēcī, perfectus,** *to complete, finish*
trīstis, -is, -e, *sad*	**īnfernus, -a, -um,** *of the lower world*
factus est, *he became*	

1. Multa sed nōn omnia dē Hercule ā Cornēliā nārrāta sunt.

Multa sed nōn omnia dē Hercule _____

2. Duo serpentēs ab Hercule īnfante ablātī sunt.

Duo serpentēs āb Hercule īnfante _____

3. Postquam fīliī ā patre excitātī sunt, Herculēs sē pūnīre voluit.

Postquam fīliī ā patre _____, Herculēs sē pūnīre voluit.

4. Rēx multās pictūrās ab Hercule perficī iussit.

Rēx _____ ab Hercule perficī iussit.

5. Canis trifōrmis, ā quō portae īnferōrum ēversae sunt, ab Hercule trāns rēgnum īnfernum ductus est.

Canis trifōrmis, ā quō portae īnferōrum _____, ab Hercule

_____

6. Rēx Herculem ā Cerberō edī voluit.

Rēx Herculem ā Cerberō _____

7. Quamquam Herculēs ad īnferōs dēscenderat, ā Cerberō nōn coctus erat.

Quamquam Herculēs ad īnferōs dēscenderat, ā Cerberō _____

AT DINNER

In addition to vocabulary and the story, the activities in this chapter focus on:
1. perfect passive participles used as verbal adjectives.
2. sentences with participial phrases.
3. alternative translations for participial phrases.

Vocabulary

Activity 33a Vocabulary

Study the vocabulary list on pages 202–203 alone or with a partner.

The Story

Activity 33b Vocabulary in Context

Fill in the blanks to match the English cues:

1. Convīvae olīvās _____ ēdērunt. (black)

2. Postquam _____ _____ _____, multae fābulae ā convīvīs nārrābantur. (goblets) (were filled)

3. Cūr Titus in trīclīnium tam sērō _____? (burst in)

4. Titus _____ _____ sine cūrā appropinquāvit. (his own place)

5. Omnēs convīvae porcum ā servīs _____ valdē laudāvērunt. (carved)

6. Clientibus frusta pullōrum data sunt, sed _____ convīvīs dē porcō datum est. (the rest of)

7. Cornēlius _____ Titō esse dēbet. (very angry)

8. Titus _____ cum clientibus, "Euge!" clāmāvit. (together)

9. Secundae mēnsae in trīclīnium portātae sunt in quibus fuērunt _____ et pira. (grapes)

10. Post cēnam clientēs cibum ā convīvīs nōn _____ in mappīs auferent. (eaten).

Building the Meaning

Perfect Passive Participles I

Activity 33c Participial Phrases

Fill in the blank in each of the following sentences with the perfect passive participle of the verb in parentheses to form a participial phrase. Make the participle agree with the italicized noun in gender, case, and number, and underline the phrase of which it is a part. Then translate the sentence. The first one is done for you:

1. *Ōrnāmenta* ē fenestrīs *ēiecta* _____ in viam cecidērunt. (ēicere)

   <u>*The furnishings thrown from the windows fell into the street.*</u> _____

2. Cornēlia, ubi *mulierem* flammīs _____ videt, commovētur. (opprimere)

   _____

3. Cornēlius *senātōrēs* ad cēnam _____ cōmiter salūtābat. (invītāre)

   _____

4. *Servī* in urbem ā dominā _____ pānem et holera comparāvērunt. (mittere)

   _____

5. Aurēlia *glīrēs* ā coquō _____ dīligenter īnspicit. (parāre)

   _____

6. Servus *soleās* ā convīvīs _____ dīligenter custōdit. (dēpōnere)

   _____

7. Cornēlius omnibus *convīvīs* in trīclīnium _____, "Accumbite," inquit, "in hīs lectīs." (dūcere)

   _____

8. Servī *porcum* ā Pseudolō _____ in trīclīnium portant. (emere)

   _____

9. *Coquus* ā Cornēliō _____ ē culīnā festīnāvit. (vocāre)

   _____

10. Convīvae in *mappīs* sēcum _____ cibum auferent. (ferre)

_____

Activity 33d Alternative Translations for Participial Phrases

Sentences with perfect participles can be translated using relative clauses or clauses introduced by **when**, **after**, *or* **since**. *Translate each of the sentences below using a clause. Consider the rest of the sentence in order to select an appropriate connector. There may be several possibilities.*

1. Cornēlia ā mātre vocāta in cubiculum festīnāvit.

_____

_____

2. Flammae ā Cornēliā vīsae multōs incolās oppressērunt.

_____

3. Pseudolus pretium ā laniō petītum dare nōn vult.

_____

4. Fābula ā Syrō nārrāta puerōs valdē dēlectāvit.

_____

5. Servī cibum ā convīvīs relictum celeriter auferunt.

_____

_____

6. Coquus ā Cornēliō laudātus in culīnam laetus rediit.

_____

Applying What You Have Learned

Activity 33e Writing the Language

Translate the following English sentences into Latin. Include all long marks. Use the stories and vocabulary lists in your textbook, as well as the vocabulary lists in this book, to help you. Use a participial phrase in each sentence:

1. The guests invited to dinner were waiting for Cornelius in the atrium.

_____

2. The guests, having been led into the dining room by slaves, reclined on couches.

_____

3. Syra and Phrygia, when ordered by Cornelius, carried water to the guests.

_____

4. The huge pig placed in the middle of the table delighted the clients.

_____

5. The guests praised the dormice bought by Aurelia herself.

_____

Activity 33f Expanding Your English Vocabulary

For each italicized English word below, give the related Latin word and below it the meaning of that Latin word. Then complete each sentence by filling in a word at the right:

Latin Word
Meaning of the Latin Word   **If you ...**

1. _____   make a *nasal* sound, you
                                          make a sound through
_____   your _____.   _____

2. _____   pick *edible* berries, you
                                          have berries that can be   _____
_____

3. _____   add a *complement* to a meal,
                                          you add something that
_____   _____ it.   _____

4. _____   choose a *location* to meet,
                                          you choose a _____   _____
_____   for the meeting.

5. _____   use a pair of *scissors*, you
                                          use a tool designed to   _____
_____

6. _____   fall victim to *pestilence*, you
                                          have a contagious _____   _____
_____   such as bubonic plague.

Activity 33g Reading Latin

*Look at the new vocabulary beneath this story. Then read the story, noting the use of perfect passive participles. Reread the story for comprehension. Then mark whether each statement about the story is V = **Vērum** (True) or F = **Falsum** (False):*

The Land of the Dead

Dum servī secundās mēnsās afferēbant, amīcus quīdam Cornēliī ūnā cum proximō convīvā pictūrās in parietibus pīctās spectābat. "Quam pulchrae," inquit convīva, nōmine Abbōnius Mucrūbius, quī amīcus Cornēliī Numidicus erat, "sunt hae pictūrae! In Āfricā domūs nostrae Numidicae tālibus pictūrīs nōn saepe ōrnātae sunt."

"In pictūrīs fābulae deōrum et hērōum nārrārī solent," respondit amīcus Cornēliī, nōmine Balbus. "Fābulae in hōc pariete dēpīctae nōbīs dē īnferīs nārrant, in quibus habitant mortuī. Domūs cīvium praeclārōrum tālēs pictūrās in multīs parietibus pīctās habēre solent."

Abbōnius mōnstrāvit pictūram in quā fuit senex palliō sordidō indūtus, quī capillōs albōs et oculōs īrātōs habēbat. "Quis est ille homō miser?" rogāvit.

Balbus respondit, "Ille est horribilis portitor, nōmine Charōn, quī mortuōs ad īnferōs fert. Eī nōn licet vīventēs ad īnferōs in scaphā eius afferre. Valdē īrātus est vīventibus quī ad īnferōs in scaphā trānsīre temptant. Paucī hominēs vīventēs in scaphā Charōnis ad īnferōs trānsiērunt. In illā pictūrā Herculēs ā rēge quōdam iussus Cerberum, illum canem īnfernum, ex īnferīs extrahit. In illā pictūrā est Orpheus, quī uxōrem in īnferīs inventam ēdūcere temptāvit. Paucī aliī vīventēs ā Charōne invītō īrātōque ad īnferōs allātī sunt."

"Quī sunt illī miserī quī ad Charōnem prōcēdunt?" rogāvit Abbōnius.

"Sunt mortuōrum umbrae, quae ā deō Mercuriō ad Charōnem adductae sunt. Eīs necesse est pecūniam Charōnī dare; in ōre igitur omnium mortuōrum pōnitur nummus. Umbrae miserae sunt quod trāns Stygem portātae terrās domūsque relictās numquam posteā vidēbunt. Semper in tenebrīs habitābunt."

Paulisper silentium erat. Deinde Abbōnius pōculum vīnō complētum sūmpsit

et, "Nunc tempus est nōbīs vīventibus bibere et cēnāre."

"Carpe diem, mī amīce," respondit Balbus.

pingō, pingere, pīnxī, pīctus, *to paint*
hērō, hērōis, m., *hero*
dēpingō, dēpingere, dēpīnxī, dēpīctus, *to depict, portray*
capillī, capillōrum, m. pl., *hair*
albus, -a, -um, *white*
portitor, portitōris, m., *ferryman*
vīvēns, vīventis, m., *living*; as substantive, *a living person*
scapha, -ae, f., *small boat*
trānseō, trānsīre, trānsiī or **trānsīvī, transitus**, *to cross, pass over*
rēx, rēgis, m., *king*
īnfernus, -a, -um, *infernal, of the lower world*
ōs, ōris, n., *mouth*
nummus, nummī, m., *coin*
Styx, Stygis, f., *the river Styx (in the underworld)*
tenebrae, tenebrārum, f. pl., *darkness*
carpō, carpere, carpsī, carptus, *to pluck, seize*

1. Spectāvērunt Balbus et Abbōnius pictūrās quae in parietibus trīclīniī pīctae erant. V F

2. Charōn pallium album gerit et capillōs sordidōs habet. V F

3. Ubi hominēs nōndum mortuī Charōnī appropinquant, portitor īrātus est. V F

4. Rēx quīdam Herculem īnferōs intrāre et Orpheum efferre iussit. V F

5. Orpheus canem amātum in īnferīs invenīre voluit. V F

6. Mercurius mortuōs ad Charōnem dūcere solet. V F

7. Mortuī nummum in ōre positum Charōnī dant. V F

THE COMISSATIO

In addition to vocabulary and the story, the activities in this chapter focus on:
1. regular comparative and superlative forms of adjectives.
2. irregular comparative and superlative forms of adjectives.

Vocabulary

Activity 34a Vocabulary

Study the vocabulary list on pages 204–205 alone or with a partner. Go to the corresponding list on the Companion website where you will find regular and irregular comparative and superlative adjectives and all the 3rd declension adjectives that you have met so far.

The Story

Activity 34b Comprehension

Complete the sentences on the left with the appropriate words, phrases, and clauses on the right. There are more words, phrases, and clauses than you will need:

1. Convīvae _____ induērunt.

2. Titus _____ rosās et unguenta poposcit.

3. Messalla arbiter bibendī esse nōn dēbuit, _____.

4. Gāius arbiter bibendī esse dēbuit, _____.

5. Necesse est rēctē arbiter bibendī creāre, _____.

6. Prīmum _____ ā Gāiō iactus est.

7. Ab alterō ē convīvīs _____ iactus est.

8. Titus tālōs magnā cum cūrā in fritillō positōs vehementer mōvit et _____ iēcit.

9. Postquam Titus arbiter bibendī creātus est _____.

10. Titus _____ ē triclīniō ablātus est.

a. canis

b. corōnās rosārum aut hederae aut flōrum

c. "Bene tibi Aurēlia!"

d. ēbrius collāpsus

e. tālī igitur cum fritillō allātī sunt

f. pōculum suum statim complēvit

g. quī multum vīnum in popīnā iam biberat

h. quod aquam modo bibēbat

i. quamquam vīnum erat pessimum

j. quod erat omnium prūdentissimus

k. sēniō

l. Venerem

Forms

Comparative and Superlative Adjectives

Activity 34c Comparisons

Translate the following sentences that contain comparatives and superlatives:

1. Praedōnēs scelestissimī erant.

_____

2. Titus erat fēlīcior quam cēterī convīvae quod Venerem iēcit.

_____

3. Sed nōn erat prūdentior quam cēterī quod statim nimis vīnī bibit.

_____

4. Crās Titus miserrimus omnium erit.

_____

5. Quam stultus est Titus! Nēmō īrātior quam Cornēlius est.

_____

6. Illud pōculum est ēlegantius quam hoc.

_____

7. Stola nova quam gerit Aurēlia pulchrior quam stolae aliārum fēminārum est.

_____

_____

8. Nōnne poēta Catullus celebrior quam Mārtiālis est?

_____

9. Aedificia Rōmānōrum ēlegantiōra quam Britannōrum erant.

_____

10. Glīrēs āb hōc mercātōre vēnditī pinguiōrēs sunt quam aliī glīrēs.

_____

Activity 34d Irregular Comparatives and Superlatives

Complete the Latin sentences to match the English cues:

1. Coquus cēnam _____ parāvit. (very good)

2. Convīvae _____ porcō dēlectābantur. (rather large)

3. Māla quae _____ erant in trīclīnium nōn allāta sunt. (too small)

4. Titus amīcō _____ in popīnā occurrerat. (rather bad)

5. Illa erat _____ omnium popīnārum. (worst)

6. "Numquam convīvam _____ vīdī," mussāvit Cornēlius. (worse)

7. Titus _____ pōculum arripuit et nimis vīnī bibit. (bigger)

8. _____ convīvārum prūdenter bibēbant. (Most)

9. "Eī semper pōculum _____ dare dēbēs," mussāvit ūnus ē convīvīs. (smallest)

10. Quamquam frāter Cornēliī vīnō oppressus est, convīvae tamen _____ grātiās Cornēliō ēgērunt. (very great)

Applying What You Have Learned

Activity 34e Writing the Language

Translate the following English sentences into Latin. Include all long marks. Use the stories and vocabulary lists in your textbook, as well as the vocabulary lists in this book, to help you:

1. The very good dinner prepared by the cook pleased Cornelius very much.

_____

2. The banquet had been prepared with the greatest care, and so the host and his guests were very happy.

_____

3. Cornelius was the wiser brother.

_____

4. Few friends of Titus will ever say, "Titus is the wisest of all!"

_____

5. Not even Cornelius wanted to allow the wine to be mixed by his brother, but he said nothing although he was becoming very angry.

_____

Activity 34f Expanding Your English Vocabulary

Many English words can be traced back to the following Latin adjectives and their irregular comparative and superlative forms. Using an English dictionary as necessary, find and write definitions of each of the English words below:

1. bonus, melior, optimus

  a. bonanza _____

  b. bonbon _____

  c. bonus _____

  d. debonair _____

  e. ameliorate _____

  f. optimist _____

  g. optimum _____

2. malus, peior, pessimus

  a. malady _____

  b. malediction _____

  c. malice _____

  d. malign (verb) _____; (adjective) _____

  e. dismal _____

  f. pejorative _____

3. magnus, maior, maximus

  a. magnanimous _____

  b. magnate _____

  c. magnify _____

    d. major (any one definition) _____

    e. majority _____

    f. maxim _____

    g. maximum _____

4. parvus, minor, minimus

    a. minor _____

    b. minus _____

    c. minimize _____

5. multus (multī), plūs (plūrēs), plūrimus

    a. multiple _____

    b. multiply _____

    c. multitude _____

    d. plural_____

    e. plurality _____

_____

Activity 34g Reading Latin

Look at the new vocabulary following this story. Then read the Latin of the story, noting comparative and superlative adjectives. Reread the Latin for comprehension. Then correct the statements about the story by rewriting them:

Further Reflections after Dinner

Aurēlia: Cūr cēterī convīvae Titum arbitrum bibendī creāvērunt?

Cornēlius: Frātrem meum maximē amant quod hilarissimus omnium semper est. Quis ē convīvīs praeter Titum arbiter bibendī fierī potuit? Praetereā tālīs arbiter bibendī creātus est.

Aurēlia: Quis ē convīvīs magis ēbrius quam Titus erat? Sērō ad cēnam vēnit et plūs vīnī bibit quam cēterī! Pōculum, ut vīdī, ē manū omīsit neque sē excūsāvit.

Nē sollicitus quidem erat atque etiam rīdēbat. Fortasse Titus hilarior quam cēterī est; aliī tamen convīvae prūdentiōrēs sunt. Nimis vīnī semper bibit Titus; pessimus igitur convīva est. Quid est peius quam imprūdēns arbiter bibendī quī plūs vīnī semper poscit?

Cornēlius: Vēra dīcis, mea carissima. Titus saepe molestissimus est sed, mihi crēde, plūrimīs convīvīs semper placet.

Aurēlia: Atque puerī trīclīniō appropinquāre vetitī prope iānuam trīclīniī stābant et convīvās spectābant neque in culīnā ūnā cum Cornēliā mānsērunt postquam cēnam ēdērunt, ut eōs iusserāmus. Quam molestissimī hāc nocte fuērunt!

Cornēlius: Ego certē īrātissimus eram. Sextus ā mē pūniētur nisi mihi pārēbit. Ille in diēs difficilior fit.

Aurēlia: Sextus sine dubiō fuit auctor malī. Noster Mārcus est melior quam Sextus; semper tibi pāret. Illōs convīvās celeberrimōs, quōs ad cēnam invītāvistī, vidēre voluit.

Cornēlius: Hāc nocte tamen puer maior minōrī puerō simillimus erat. Ēheu! Puerōs et Titum ad vīllam rūsticam ūnā cum servīs scelestissimīs remittere volō.

hilaris, -is, -e, *cheerful*, *merry*
omittō, omittere, omīsī, omissus, *to drop*, *let slip*
imprūdēns, imprūdentis, *foolish*, *imprudent*
pāreō, -ēre, -uī, -itūrus + dat., *to obey*
auctor, auctōris, m., *originator*
remittō, remittere, remīsī, remissus, *to send back*

1. Cēterī convīvae Titum virum prūdentissimum amant.

_____

2. Aliī convīvae magis ēbriī quam Titus erant.

_____

_____

3. Quod Titus plūrimum vīnum bibit, melior convīva quam cēterī est.

_____

4. Minimus arbiter bibendī est convīva quī plūs vīnī semper poscit.

_____

5. Puerī erant suāvissimī quod trīclīniō appropinquāvērunt.

_____

6. Sextus est melior quam Mārcus.

_____

7. Convīvae quīdam procācissimī ad cēnam īnvītāti erant et eōs vidēre voluit Mārcus.

_____

CRIME

> *In addition to vocabulary and the story, the activities in this chapter focus on:*
> 1. comparisons with **quam** and with the ablative of comparison.
> 2. the ablative of degree of difference
> 3. positive, comparative, and superlative adverbs

Web Code: jgd-0008

Vocabulary

Activity 35a Vocabulary

Study the vocabulary list on page 206 alone or with a partner. Go to the corresponding list on the Companion website where you will find regular and irregular positive, comparative, and superlative adverbs.

The Story

Activity 35b Vocabulary in Context

Fill in the blanks with Latin words to match the English cues:

1. Eucleidēs domum per Subūram _____ ambulābat. (too slowly)

2. Baculum quō Eucleidēs _____ sē dēfendēbat ā praedōnibus

   _____ _____

   _____. (very bravely) (easily) (from him) (was taken away)

3. Eucleidēs _____ _____ ab alterō praedōne

   _____ _____. (from the back) (was grabbed)

4. Eucleidēs fūste _____ ad terram cecidit. (having been struck)

5. Praedōnēs omnem pecūniam _____ _____. (from him)
   (took away)

6. Eucleidēs noster _____ _____ accēpit. (a very serious
   wound)

7. Ubi Eucleidem vīdit, "_____ _____!" exclāmāvit
   Cornēlius. (Good heavens!)

8. Corpus Eucleidis fuit _____ _____. (sprinkled with
   blood)

9. Servī ā Cornēliō vocātī _____ _____ in ātrium concurrērunt. (as quickly as possible)

10. Vulnera Eucleidis ā servīs _____ _____

    _____. (very carefully) (were bound up)

11. Quamquam prīmum Eucleidēs poētae Mārtiālī _____

    _____, nunc tamen eī _____. (did not believe) (believes)

Building the Meaning

Comparisons

Activity 35c Making Comparisons

Rewrite each of the following sentences, changing the comparison with **quam** *to the ablative of comparison or vice versa, as in the example below:*

Mārtiālis est prūdentior quam Eucleidēs.

Mārtiālis est prūdentior Eucleide.

1. Titus est arbiter bibendī melior quam Messalla.

   Titus est arbiter bibendī _____.

2. Titus erat fēlīcior quam cēterī convīvae quod Venerem iēcit.

   Titus erat _____ quod Venerem iēcit.

3. Pseudolus procācior quam lanius erat.

   Pseudolus _____ erat.

4. Porcī pinguiōrēs quam canēs quīdam sunt.

   Porcī _____ sunt.

5. Fercula in quibus erat gustātiō erant multō grāviōra quam illa in quibus carō erat.

   Fercula in quibus erat gustātiō erant _____ in quibus carō erat.

6. Hoc aedificium est multō īnfirmius illō.

   Hoc aedificium est _____.

7. Praedōnēs celeriōrēs Eucleide erant.

Praedōnēs _____ erant.

8. Mārcus erat fortior Sextō. Itaque lupum repellere poterat.

Mārcus erat _____. Itaque lupum repellere poterat.

9. Tuī albātī peiōrēs meīs russātīs heri in Cīrcō Maximō erant.

Tuī albātī _____ heri in Cīrcō Maximō erant.

10. Fōrum Rōmānum veterius Amphitheātrō Flāviō est.

Fōrum Rōmānum _____ est.

Forms

Adverbs: Positive

Activity 35d Forming Positive Adverbs

In each of the following pairs of sentences, form a positive adverb from the italicized adjective in the first sentence and write the adverb in the blank in the second sentence. Then translate both sentences. The first one is done for you:

1. Cornēlia *bonum* librum legit. Cornēlia <u>bene</u> legere potest.

   <u>*Cornelia is reading a good book. Cornelia can read well.*</u>

2. Eucleidēs vulnera *gravia* accēpit. Eucleidēs _____ vulnerātus est.

   _____

3. Syrus fābulam *brevem* puerīs nārrat. Syrus puerīs dē Pseudolō _____ nārrat.

   _____

4. Bovēs *tardī* plaustra trahunt. Bovēs plaustra _____ trahunt.

   _____

5. Cornēlius servōs *dīligentēs* habet. Cēna ā servīs _____ parātur.

   _____

6. Quam *fortis* est Eucleidēs! Eucleidēs baculō _____ sē dēfendit.

_____

7. Viae sunt plēnae praedōnum *scelestōrum*. Viātōrēs ā praedōnibus _____ petuntur.

_____

Adverbs: Positive, Comparative, and Superlative

Activity 35e Forming Comparative and Superlative Adverbs

Fill in the blank in each of the following sentences with the form of the adverb indicated in parentheses. Then translate the sentence:

1. Eucleidēs _____ domum redierat. (**sērō**, superlative)

_____

2. Cornēlia ā miserīs līberīs _____ commovētur. (**magnopere**, superlative)

_____

3. Eucleidēs apud frātrem _____ mānsit. (**diū**, superlative)

_____

4. Titus _____ clientibus advēnit. (**sērō**, comparative)

_____

5. Gāius vīnum _____ quam Titus miscēbit. (**prūdenter**, comparative)

_____

6. Quamquam Eucleidēs quam _____ ambulābat, praedōnēs eum

_____ cōnsecūtī sunt. (**celeriter**, superlative) (**facile**, superlative)

_____

7. Cornēlius vīnum _____ quam frāter bibit. (**lentē**, comparative)

_____

8. Titus _____ ēbrius Cornēliō fit. (**magnopere**, comparative)

_____

Applying What You Have Learned

Activity 35f Writing the Language

Translate the following English sentences into Latin. Include all long marks. Use the stories and vocabulary lists in your textbook, as well as the vocabulary lists in this book, to help you:

1. Eucleides, having been struck fiercely with a very big club, finally arrived home very late.

_____

_____

2. Cornelius was rather worried, because Eucleides' tunic was very dirty and sprinkled with blood.

_____

_____

3. "You have been rather seriously wounded," said Cornelius, and he ordered the wounds to be bound as quickly as possible.

_____

_____

4. The slaves were placing Eucleides on the couch. Cornelius, greatly affected by this sight, said, "Move him more carefully!"

_____

_____

5. Cornelius then said to Eucleides very sadly, "You certainly were most brave, Eucleides, but very foolish."

_____

_____

Activity 35g Expanding Your English Vocabulary

Using the word bank below, write the word that could replace the italicized word or words in each sentence. Use the Latin words in parentheses to help determine the meaning of the English words. Then write the English translation of each Latin word in the word bank:

1. When he fell, Eucleides could have torn a *fibrous tissue* that ties bones together.   _____

2. Syrus drives the coach with great *ease* and skill.   _____

3. By walking alone at night, Eucleides made himself *exposed to being injured*.   _____

4. Eucleides' story was shocking and *unbelievable*.   _____

5. When he was struck, Eucleides fell *face-down* in the mud.   _____

6. Although his wounds were *serious*, Eucleides soon recovered.   _____

7. Eucleides' decision to walk alone at night was not very *wise*.   _____

8. To get to his brother's house, Eucleides had to travel to the *top* of the Quirinal Hill.   _____

9. Before this episode, Eucleides was not a *fearful* man.   _____

10. Aurelia did not feel *safe* spending the night in an inn.   _____

facility (**facile**) _____	secure (**sēcūrus**) _____
timorous (**timor**) _____	prone (**prōnus**) _____
ligament (**ligāre**) _____	prudent (**prūdēns**) _____
summit (**summus**) _____	vulnerable (**vulnus**) _____
grave (**gravis**) _____	incredible (**crēdere**) _____

Activity 35h Reading Latin

*Look at the new vocabulary beneath this story. Then read the Latin of the story, noting comparative and superlative adverbs, the use of **quam** in comparisons, and the ablative of degree of difference. Reread the Latin for comprehension. Then match the first part of each sentence that follows to the phrase or clause that correctly completes it:*

Kitchen Gossip

Postrīdiē variī rūmōrēs ad aurēs servōrum pervēnērunt. "Quid," inquiunt, "Eucleidī nostrō heri nocte accidit? Hodiē gravissimē aegrōtat neque puerōs ad lūdum dūcere potest. Frātremne vīsitābat? Ībatne per Subūram sōlus? Nōs omnēs illam partem huius urbis vītāre solēmus quod Subūra est sordidissima et multō perīculōsior quam hic collis."

Multī ē servīs Eucleidem domum sērius redeuntem vīderant et eum adiūverant, sed nēmō nisi Macedō, amīcus eius, rem ipsam miserrimam audīverat. Ille igitur servīs cēterīs rem tōtam nārrāvit.

"Eucleidēs noster," inquit, "dum heri māne in urbem dēscendit, poētae cuidam clārissimō occurrit. Ad īnsulam ubi frāter habitat cum poētā ambulāvit. Ille poēta, cui nōmen est Mārtiālis, plūrima dē librīs suīs Eucleidī nārrāvit. Multa quoque dē praedōnibus scelestissimīs monuit, sed Eucleidēs eī nōn crēdidit.

"Apud frātrem diūtissimē manēbat neque dē praedōnibus cōgitābat. Dum tamen mediā nocte domum redit, duo hominēs ignōtī subitō ē popīnā ērūpērunt. Eucleidēs celerius ambulābat sed frūstrā, nam praedōnēs eum facillimē cōnsecūtī sunt. 'Trāde nōbīs pecūniam!' ferōcissimē clāmāvērunt. 'Nisi pecūniam nōbīs dederis, tē necābimus.'

"Amīcus noster nihil respondit sed sē baculō fortissimē dēfendēbat. Tum illī praedōnēs eum oppugnāvērunt et fūstibus percussērunt. Mox Eucleidēs prōnus in lutō iacēbat et paulisper immōbilis mortem simulābat quod valdē timēbat. Illī pecūniam amīcō nostrō adēmērunt atque rīdentēs abiērunt.

"Hodiē aeger in lectō iacet. Quis est miserior et īnfēlicior Eucleide nostrō? Nocte in Subūram sōlus īre nōn dēbuit, nam in eā urbis parte nē mīlitēs quidem sōlī ambulāre solent."

varius, -a, -um, *different*, *various*, *varied*

auris, auris, gen. pl., **aurium**, f., *ear*

aegrōtō, -āre, -āvī, -ātūrus, *to be ill*

rediēns, redeuntis, *returning*

clārus, -a, -um, *bright*, *famous*

moneō, -ēre, -uī, -itus, *to warn*

ignōtus, -a, -um, *unknown*, *strange*

ērumpō, ērumpere, ērūpī, ēruptus, *to burst out*

oppugnō, -āre, -āvī, -ātus, *to attack*

aeger, aegra, aegrum, *ill*

īnfēlīx, īnfēlīcis, *unhappy*, *unlucky*

1. Eucleidēs fatuus fuit quod . . . _____

2. Eucleidēs fābulam suam amīcō Macedonī nārrāvit ubi . . . _____

3. Eucleidēs nōn crēdidit poētae Mārtiālī quī . . . _____

4. Quod Eucleidēs diūtius apud frātrem mānserat . . . _____

5. Eucleidem cōnsecūtī sunt praedōnēs quī . . . _____

6. Eucleidēs sē baculō fortissimē dēfendit sed . . . _____

7. Dum Eucleidēs immōbilis iacet . . . _____

a. praedōnēs fortiōrēs fuērunt.

b. sērius ē domō frātris discessit.

c. praedōnēs pecūniam adēmērunt.

d. domum mediā nocte sōlus ambulāvit.

e. multō prūdentior dē praedōnibus fuit.

f. domum sērius rediit.

g. multō celerius miserō servō currere potuērunt.

A Letter

Go Online
PHSchool.com
Web Code: jgd-0009

In addition to vocabulary and the story, the activities for this chapter focus on:
1. conversion of our dates to Roman dates.
2. different uses of **quam**.

Vocabulary

Activity 36a Vocabulary

Study the vocabulary list on pages 207–208 alone or with a partner. Go to the corresponding list on the Companion website where you will find a list of the uses of **quam**.

The Story

Activity 36b Story Comprehension

Pretend you are Flavia and write in English a reply to Cornelia's letter. Include responses to what Cornelia says in each of the paragraphs of her letter. Write your letter on a separate sheet of paper.

Forms

Dates

Activity 36c Practice with Dates

Give the dates for the following, first according to the English system and then according to the Roman system:

1. The first day of school this year _____ _____

2. Halloween _____ _____

3. Veterans' Day _____ _____

4. Thanksgiving _____ _____

5. Saturnalia _____ _____

6. Groundhog Day _____ _____

7. Valentine's Day _____ _____

8. The first day of spring _____ _____

9. The first day of summer _____ _____

10. Independence Day _____ _____

Building the Meaning

Translating *quam*

Activity 36d Identifying Uses of *quam*

Identify the use of **quam** *in each of the following sentences by writing one of the following numbers on the line at the right. Then translate the italicized words:*

1. in a comparison   3. in an exclamation   5. in a relative clause
2. in a phrase with a superlative   4. in a question

1. *Quam lentē* haec aestās Rōmae praeterit! _____

_____ this summer is going past in Rome!

2. *Epistula quam pater meus heri accēpit* Brundisiī scrīpta est. _____

_____ was written in Brundisium.

3. Pater meus epistulam hodiē scrībit. *Quam celeriter tabellārius hanc epistulam ad Valerium feret?* _____

My father is writing a letter today. _____

_____

4. *Eucleidēs apud frātem quam diutissimē mānsit* quod uxor frātris optimam cēnam parāverat. _____

because his brother's wife had prepared a very good dinner.

5. Eucleidēs, quod praedōnēs quīdam eum sequēbantur, *quam celerrimē currēbat.* _____

Eucleidēs, because certain robbers were following him, _____

_____

6. *Praedōnēs tamen celerius quam Eucleidēs currere poterant,* quod Eucleidēs currere nōn solēbat. _____

because Eucleides was not accustomed to running.

7. *Quam scelestī erant illī hominēs*, quī Eucleidī nostrō nocuērunt!   _____

_____ who hurt our Eucleides!

8. *Palla quam māter mihi ēmit* pulcherrima est.   _____

_____ is very beautiful.

Applying What You Have Learned

Activity 36e Writing the Language

Translate the following English sentences into Latin. Include all long marks. Use the stories and vocabulary lists in your textbook, as well as the vocabulary lists in this book, to help you:

1. In the year A.D. 80 the emperor was Titus Flavius Vespasian, who was much wiser than Nero.

_____

_____

2. Cornelius, ordered to return to Rome by the emperor, departed from the country house on August 28 along with his wife and children.

_____

_____

3. How sad Cornelia was because she left her best friend, Flavia!

_____

_____

4. How diligent are the slaves and slave-women? They are working as diligently as possible.

_____

_____

5. On November 3, Gaius Cornelius read the letter sent by Valerius.

_____

_____

Activity 36f Expanding Your English Vocabulary

Using the word bank that follows, write the word that could replace the italicized word or words in each sentence. Use the Latin words in parentheses to help determine the meaning of the English words. Then write the English translation of each Latin word in the word bank:

1. Marcus is in his *teenage years.* _____

2. The earliest Roman *listing of the months in the year* contained only ten months. _____

3. Cornelia hopes Flavia will *convince* her father to bring her to Rome. _____

4. Eucleides' decision to walk alone through the city at night was *bold* but unwise. _____

5. The *seventh month* of the year was renamed for Caesar. _____

6. Rome's first emperor gave his name to the *eighth month.* _____

July (**Iūlius**) _____   calendar (**Kalendae**) _____

adolescence (**adulēscēns**) _____   persuade (**persuādēre**) _____

audacious (**audāx**) _____   August (**Augustus**) _____

Activity 36g Reading Latin

Look at the new vocabulary beneath this story. Then read the story, noting uses of **quam**. *Reread the story for comprehension. Then answer the questions that follow with complete Latin sentences:*

The Morning After

Nōnīs Novembribus māne surrēxērunt omnēs praeter Eucleidem, quī propter vulnera adhūc aegrōtābat et in lectō manēbat. Cornēlia in cubiculō sedēns respondēbat epistulae quam Flāvia Kalendīs Novembribus scrīpserat. Aurēlia puerōs in ātrium vocāverat. "Pater tuus, Mārce," inquit, "ad Cūriam discessit."

Cui Mārcus, "Ubi est patruus meus? Nōnne apud nōs, ut solet, pernoctāvit?"

Aurēlia respondit, "Titus domum redīre voluit."

"Sine dubiō," interpellāvit Sextus cum rīsū, "caput eī hodiē maximē dolet quod heri plūs vīnī quam cēterī bibit et ēbrius domum discessit."

"Nōlī tam procāx esse, Sexte!" clāmāvit Aurēlia īrāta. "In diēs molestior fīs. Agite, puerī! In animō habeō vōs ūnā cum servō mittere ad lībertum nostrum quī in īnsulā prope domum Titī habitat. Ille lībertus est senex atque īnfirmus. Itaque aliquid pullī ad eum mittere volō. Servus ad iānuam vōs iam exspectat. Discēdite quam celerrimē."

Brevī tempore puerī ad illam īnsulam pervēnērunt. Ibi in cēnāculō habitābat lībertus Cornēliī cum uxōre et septem līberīs. Tum Mārcus, "Prīmum ad quīntum tabulātum ascendere necesse est; deinde Titum, patruum meum, quī in domō vīcīnā habitat, vīsitābimus."

Erant scālae multae et arduae et obscūrae. Tandem ad cēnāculum vix pervēnērunt. Servus iānuam pulsāvit. Iānuam aperuit lībertī uxor; eī cibus trāditus est. Puerī stābant ad iānuam, per quam parvum lībertī cēnāculum et līberōs vidēre poterant. "Quam sordidum est cēnāculum!" exclāmāvit Mārcus. "Nōn sine maximā difficultāte aqua cibusque hūc afferrī possunt. Quam īnfēlīcēs līberī sunt! Sine aquā vīvere nōn possunt." At Sextus rīdēns, "Quam fēlīcēs līberī sunt! Sine aquā sē lavāre nōn possunt."

Puerī in viam dēscendērunt. Rīsum tumultumque maximum subitō audīvērunt. "Quid est?" rogāvit Sextus. "Ecce! Virī, līberī, mulierēs ante illam iānuam stant. Quid spectant?"

Puerī ad iānuam festīnāvērunt. Rem mīram cōnspexērunt: in ipsō līmine stertēns iacēbat Titus!

caput eī...dolet, *he has a headache*	**scālae, -ārum,** f. pl., *stairs*
fīs, *you become*	**arduus, -a, -um,** *steep*
senex, senis, m., *old man*	**pulsō, -āre, -āvī, -ātus,** *to strike, knock on*
cēnāculum, -ī, n., *upper room, garret*	**līmen, līminis,** n., *threshold, doorway*

1. Quō diē Flāvia epistulam Cornēliae scrīpserat?

_____

2. Quid Titus post cēnam apud Cornēlium facere solet?

_____

3. Quid ad lībertum ferent puerī?

_____

4. Quōcum puerī ad īnsulam lībertī iērunt?

_____

5. Quis in īnsulā quae erat prope domum Titī habitābat?

_____

6. Cūr difficillimum erat ad cēnāculum lībertī cibum et aquam afferre?

_____

7. Quid spectant virī et līberī et mulierēs?

_____

OFF TO SCHOOL

Web Code: jgd-0010

> *In addition to vocabulary and the story, the activities for this chapter focus on:*
> 1. deponent verbs.
> 2. discriminating between deponent verbs and passive forms of regular verbs.

Vocabulary

Activity 37a Vocabulary

Study the vocabulary list on page 209 and the corresponding list on the Companion website.

The Story

Activity 37b Vocabulary in Context

Fill in the blanks with Latin words to match the English cues (use deponent verbs wherever possible):

1. _____ puerīs necesse est ad lūdum _____. (Every day)
   (to set out)

2. "Ille _____ in diēs peior fit," cōgitābat Sextus. (school)

3. Puerī cum _____ _____ per viās ambulābant.
   (very learned tutor)

4. Lanterna puerīs ab Eucleide _____. (was being carried in front of)

5. Ubi puerī iēntāculum sūmpsērunt, ē pīstrīnō _____, et invītī ad lūdum
   ambulābant. (went out)

6. Eucleidēs rēs _____ quam versūs Vergiliī docet. (more useful)

7. "Quam laetus," inquit Eucleidēs, "ille _____ vōs accipiet!"
   (secondary school teacher)

8. Eucleidēs celerius quam puerī semper _____. (talks)

9. "Nisi statim in lūdum _____, puerī," inquit grammaticus, "ā mē

   _____." (you enter/will have entered) (you will be reprimanded)

10. "Ego tamen nec illum grammaticum nec illōs versūs Vergiliī _____."
    (will fear)

11. "Fortasse _____ illōrum versuum Vergiliī hodiē legēmus." (a small amount)

12. "Hodiē, etiamsī aliī dormient, ego omnia audīre _____." (will try)

Forms

Deponent Verbs

Activity 37c Common Deponent Verbs

In the space after each verb in the left-hand columns, write the letter of the verb in the right-hand columns that has the same or nearly the same meaning:

1. intrāverat _____   8. manēbam _____   **a.** proficīscētur   **h.** expertī sunt

2. dīxit _____   9. intrātis _____   **b.** loquēbāmur   **i.** locūtus est

3. discēdet _____   10. mānserāmus _____   **c.** profectus es   **j.** veritus sum

4. timent _____   11. dīcis _____   **d.** morābar   **k.** morātī erāmus

5. intrāvistis _____   12. timuī _____   **e.** loqueris   **l.** ingrediminī

6. discessistī _____   13. temptant _____   **f.** ingressus erat   **m.** ingressī estis

7. temptāvērunt _____   14. dīcēbāmus _____   **g.** verentur   **n.** experiuntur

Activity 37d Using Deponent Verbs

In the spaces to the right of the sentences below and on page 72, write the appropriate forms of the verbs in parentheses to replace the italicized verbs in the sentences. The first one is done for you:

1. "Ego illō incendiō appropinquāre," inquit Cornēlia,

   "valdē *timuī*." (vereor)   *verita sum*

2. Diū in urbe *manēbimus*. (moror)   _____

3. In lūdō semper dīligenter labōrāre *vīs*. (cōnor)   _____

4. Praedōnēs Eucleidem celerius *petīvērunt*. (cōnsequor)   _____

5. Convīvae multa inter sē *dīcēbant*. (loquor)   _____

6. Eucleidēs vulnerātus in terram *ceciderat*. (collābor)   _____

7. Mox laetissimī ē lūdō *exībitis*. (ēgredior)   _____

8. "Heri," inquit Sextus, "ad lūdum invītus *iī*." (proficīscor)   _____

9. Cum Eucleidēs domum *redierit*, vulnera ā servīs ligābuntur. (regredior)   _____

10. In illam caupōnam *intrāre nōlumus*. (ingredior) (vereor)   _____

   _____

11. Quod iam Baiīs *discessistis*, vōs maximē dēsīderō. (proficīscor) _____

12. "Cavē, Tite," inquit Cornēlius. "In lectum *cadēs*." (collābor) _____

13. "*Intrā*, Sexte!" inquit Palaemōn. (ingredior) "Cūr extrā lūdum

    manēs?" (moror) _____

Applying What You Have Learned

Activity 37e Writing the Language

Translate the following English sentences into Latin, using deponent verbs wherever possible.
Include all long marks. Use the stories and vocabulary lists in your textbook, as well as the
vocabulary lists in this book, to help you:

1. The boys, having set out before light, were unwillingly following Eucleides to school.

   _____

   _____

2. Soon, however, they ran ahead, and Eucleides was trying very hard to catch up to them.

   _____

   _____

3. Palaemon, that most learned teacher, was waiting at the door of the school.

   _____

   _____

4. The boys were not afraid to go into the school because Palaemon greeted them courteously.

   _____

   _____

5. Having entered the school, Marcus said to Sextus, "How courteously this teacher receives us!"

   _____

   _____

6. Sextus replied to him, "Wait for a short time, Marcus. He has not tested us yet."

   _____

   _____

Name _____ Date _____ Period _____

Activity 37f Expanding Your English Vocabulary

Using the word bank below, write the word that could replace the italicized word or words in each sentence. Use the Latin words in parentheses to help determine the meaning of the English words. Then write the English translation of each Latin word in the word bank:

1. Eucleides was so *talkative*, the boys found it difficult to get a word in edgewise. _____

2. Although he was twelve years old, the boy's *backward* behavior made him appear to be much younger. _____

3. Because of a riot, a *suspension* was imposed on gladiatorial contests in Pompeii for ten years. _____

4. *Usefulness* is more important than appearance; it does not matter how good something looks if it is of no use. _____

5. Everyone was deeply moved by the senator's *well-spoken* speech. _____

6. Eucleides did not approve of the *conversational* language of the streets, and he forbade the boys to use such slang. _____

7. Eucleides preferred the *learned* language of scholars to the speech of the common people. _____

8. The *Odyssey* is a *follow-up* to the *Iliad*, since the events of the story of Odysseus follow the destruction of Troy. _____

9. "Palaemon does not use sound *teaching* techniques," complained Sextus. "I never learn anything!" _____

10. As a *result* of his lack of proper study, Sextus was unable to respond correctly when called upon in school. _____

colloquial (**loquī**) _____	erudite (**ērudītus**) _____
pedagogical (**paedagōgus**) _____	consequence (**cōnsequī**) _____
regressive (**regredī**) _____	loquacious (**loquī**) _____
utility (**ūtilis**) _____	eloquent (**loquī**) _____
sequel (**sequī**) _____	moratorium (**morārī**) _____

Activity 37g Reading Latin

Look at the new vocabulary following this story. Then read the Latin of the story, noting deponent verbs. Reread the Latin for comprehension. Then match the first part of each sentence that follows to the phrase or clause that correctly completes it:

Another Early Morning

(Mārcus et Sextus cum Eucleide iam ē domō ēgressī erant et ad lūdum profectī erant. Puerī, dum ambulābant, inter sē loquēbantur.)

Sextus:	Ecce! Taberna ubi pānem emere solēmus. Valdē ēsuriō. Nōbīsne licet pānem hodiē emere, Eucleidēs?
Eucleidēs:	Ita vērō, sed vōbīs festīnāre necesse est. Nōlīte in tabernā morārī!
Puerī:	Id pollicēmur!

(Puerī pānem ēmērunt. Dum edunt, subito vīdērunt duōs sīcāriōs quī ad carcerem ā vigilibus dūcēbantur.)

Mārcus:	Quid fēcērunt hī hominēs? Cūr in carcerem dūcuntur?
Adstāns quīdam:	Scelera admīsērunt. Sīcāriī sunt. Proximā nocte vigilēs eōs in Subūrā comprehendērunt.
Sextus:	Quam miserī videntur. Ecce! Alter sīcārius paene collāpsus est!
Eucleidēs:	Cavē, Sexte! Nōlīte illōs virōs scelestissimōs sequī.
Mārcus:	Fortasse illī erant quī tē aggressī sunt. Vel fortasse pecūniam virō dīvitī adēmērunt. Nunc captī sunt et poenās dabunt.

(Puerī et Eucleidēs iterum profectī sunt et brevī tempore ad lūdum appropinquābant.)

Mārcus:	Quid faciet hodiē grammaticus?
Sextus:	Ēheu! Semper eadem facere nōs iubet. Semper nōs plūrēs versūs recitāre iubet et nōs experītur. Semper mē castīgat quod, quamquam in lūdō vigilāre cōnor, saepissimē tamen obdormiō. Numquam ā labōre dēsistimus sed nihil discimus. Cotīdiē diū sedeō et miser sum. Ingredī in lūdum nōlō.
Mārcus:	Bonō animō es! Fortasse hodiē aliquid novī faciet grammaticus.
Sextus:	Fortasse obdormiet grammaticus ipse!

polliceor, pollicērī, pollicitus sum, *to promise*

sīcārius, -ī, m., *murderer*

carcer, carceris, m., *prison*

vigil, vigilis, m., *watchman*

scelus, sceleris, n., *crime*

admittō, admittere, admīsī, admissus, *to commit*

proximā nocte, *last night*

comprehendō, comprehendere, comprehendī, comprehēnsus, *to arrest*

aggredior, aggredī, aggressus sum, *to attack*

dīves, dīvitis, *rich*

poenās dare, *to be punished, pay the penalty*

dēsistō, dēsistere, destitī, *to leave off, cease*

discō, discere, didicī, *to learn*

es! *be!*

1. Puerī pānem emērunt neque … _____
2. Puerī in viā cōnspexērunt vigilēs quī … _____
3. Puerī in viā cōnspexērunt sīcāriōs quī … _____
4. Fortasse scelestī ā vigilibus comprehēnsī … _____
5. Quamquam Sextus in lūdō vigilāre cōnātur … _____
6. Dum sīcāriī per viam prōgrediuntur … _____
7. Cotīdiē Sextus in lūdō miser est quod … _____

a. alter paene collāpsus est.
b. Eucleidem in Subūrā aggressī erant.
c. in tabernā morātī sunt.
d. vigilēs ad carcerem sequēbantur.
e. puerī nihil in lūdō discunt neque ā labōre dēsistunt.
f. sīcāriōs ad carcerem dūcēbant.
g. saepissimē obdormit.

THE LESSONS BEGIN

Go Online
PHSchool.com
Web Code: jgd-0011

In addition to vocabulary and the story, the activities for this chapter focus on:
1. counting with cardinal numbers and ordinal numbers.
2. transforming Roman numerals to Arabic numerals.

Vocabulary

Activity 38a Vocabulary

Study the vocabulary list on pages 210–211 and the corresponding list on the Companion website.

The Story

Activity 38b Questions on the Story

Using the story at the beginning of Chapter 38 as a guide, answer the following questions in complete Latin sentences:

1. Abhinc quot mēnsēs puerī prīmum librum Aenēidis lēgērunt?

   _____

2. Quot annōs Graecī Troiam obsidēbant?

   _____

3. Quid urbī captae accidit?

   _____

4. Quī ūnā cum Aenēā ex urbe Troiā captā effūgērunt?

   _____

5. Quid petēbant?

   _____

6. Quid passī sunt Troiānī ubi ex urbe Siciliā profectī sunt?

   _____

7. Quō Aenēās āctus est?

   _____

8. Cuius ad urbem Aenēās advēnit?

_____

9. Quōmodo Dīdō Aenēān accēpit?

_____

10. Quid Aenēās in convīviō fēcit?

_____

11. Quid fēcērunt omnēs convīvae?

_____

12. Ubi Aenēās sedēbat?

_____

13. Quālem dolōrem Aenēās renovat?

_____

Forms

Numbers in Latin

Activity 38c Cardinal Numbers: Latin Math

Fill in the missing numbers, and then rewrite each equation using Roman numerals. The first set is done for you:

1. Decem + quattuor = ____*quattuordecim*____.   _X_ + _IV_ = _XIV_

2. _____ - octō = quīnque.   ____ - ____ = ____

3. Quīnquāgintā + _____ = centum.   ____ + ____ = ____

4. Quīndecim ÷ _____ = quīnque.   ____ ÷ ____ = ____

5. Duo × sex = _____.   ____ × ____ = ____

6. Decem + novem = _____.   ____ + ____ = ____

7. Vīgintī × _____ = centum.   ____ × ____ = ____

8. _____ - octō = decem.   ____ - ____ = ____

9. Quattuordecim ÷ septem = _____.   _____ ÷ _____ = _____

10. _____ × duo = duodēvīgintī.   _____ × _____ = _____

11. Sēdecim ÷ quattuor = _____.   _____ ÷ _____ = _____

Activity 38d Ordinal Numbers

Complete the following list of the months of the year. The first is done for you:

1. Aprīlis est _____*quartus*_____ mēnsis annī.

2. September est _____ mēnsis annī.

3. Māius est _____ mēnsis annī.

4. November est _____ mēnsis annī.

5. Iūnius est _____ mēnsis annī.

6. Februārius est _____ mēnsis annī.

7. Iūlius est _____ mēnsis annī.

8. Mārtius est _____ mēnsis annī.

9. Octōber est _____ mēnsis annī.

10. Augustus est _____ mēnsis annī.

11. Iānuārius est _____ mēnsis annī.

12. December est _____ mēnsis annī.

Applying What You Have Learned

Activity 38e Writing the Language

Translate the following English sentences into Latin, using deponent verbs wherever possible. Include all long marks. Use the stories and vocabulary lists in your textbook, as well as the vocabulary lists in this book, to help you:

1. How many books of the *Aeneid* are there? There are twelve. Aeneas sails from the ruins of Troy because he wants to found a new city.

_____

_____

2. In which book did the boys read about the end of the city of Troy? In the second book.

_____

3. Aeneas, having set out with twenty ships, because of a very great storm arrived in Africa with only seven.

_____

_____

4. Aeneas, having suffered much on the very long journey, was welcomed graciously by Queen Dido with his friends and son.

_____

_____

5. At what time will the students leave school? At the sixth hour they will return home.

_____

Activity 38f Connecting with Italian and French

At the left in boldface is a complete list of the cardinal numbers in Latin from one to twenty, in numerical order. Using your knowledge of the Latin numbers, deduce the meaning of each of the Italian and French numbers (in scrambled order) at the right and write the corresponding Arabic numbers (1, 2, 3, etc.) on the lines provided:

Latin	Latin	Italian		Italian		French		French	
ūnus, -a, -um	tredecim or	quattro	___	diciannove	___	deux	___	dix-neuf	___
duo, -ae, -o	decem (et)	dodici	___	sette	___	dix	___	quinze	___
	trēs	sei	___	due	___	quatre	___	seize	___
trēs, trēs, tria	quattuordecim	uno	___	quattordici	___	six	___	treize	___
quattuor	quīndecim	sedici	___	venti	___	dix-sept	___	huit	___
quīnque	sēdecim	nove	___	diciotto	___	onze	___	un	___
sex	septendecim	diciassette	___	undici	___	quatorze	___	dix-huit	___
septem	duodēvīgintī or	dieci	___	tredici	___	sept	___	trois	___
octō	octōdecim	cinque	___			cinq			
novem	undēvīgintī or	quindici	___			douze			
decem	novendecim	tre	___			neuf	___		
ūndecim	vīgintī	otto	___			vingt	___		
duodecim									

Activity 38g Expanding Your English Vocabulary

Using the word bank below, write the word that could replace the italicized word or words in each sentence. Use the Latin words in parentheses to help determine the meaning of the English words. Then write the English translation of each Latin word in the word bank:

1. The Greek philosopher Socrates had many *pupils*,
   among whom was Plato.   _____

2. The Cornelii enjoy their *yearly* vacation in Baiae.   _____

3. In ancient times, *sailing* on the Adriatic Sea in winter
   was often dangerous.   _____

4. Fish and other *sea-dwelling* creatures are abundant
   along the coast near Baiae.   _____

5. The hills of Baiae are home to many *land-dwelling*
   creatures as well.   _____

6. Aeneas was driven to the coast of Africa by a great *storm*.   _____

7. Aurelia shows little *endurance* in dealing with her servants.   _____

8. Near Baiae, a large part of the Roman *force of ships*
   is anchored.   _____

9. The relationship between Cornelius and his driver Syrus is
   sometimes *stormy*.   _____

10. Clients worry that their names might be *removed* from the
    guest list at their patron's dinner party.   _____

marine (**mare**) _____	deleted (**dēlēre**) _____
navy (**nāvis**) _____	disciples (**discipulus**) _____
annual (**annus**) _____	terrestrial (**terra**) _____
patience (**patī**) _____	tempestuous (**tempestās**) _____
tempest (**tempestās**) _____	navigation (**nāvigāre**) _____

Activity 38h Reading Latin

Look at the new vocabulary beneath this story. Then read the story, noting cardinal and ordinal numbers. Reread the Latin for comprehension. Then correct the statements following the story by filling in the blanks:

From Kings to Consuls

Grammaticus puerīs dē historiā Rōmānā locūtus est.

"Rōmānī antīquī regēbantur ā septem rēgibus, quōrum prīmus erat Rōmulus. Urbs Rōma ā Rōmulō condita est et ab eō multōs annōs bene regēbātur. Rēx secundus, Numa Pompilius, ā dīs magnopere amābātur quod ab eō templa aedificāta sunt et rēs sacrae īnstitūtae sunt.

"Tertius rēx erat Tullus Hostilius, vir ferōx, quī ab hostibus Rōmānōrum maximē timēbātur. Ab Ancō Marciō, rēge quartō, urbs Rōma aucta est atque Pōns Sublicius in Tiberī factus est.

"Inde rēgnum tenēbat vir Etruscus, Tarquinius Prīscus nōmine, ā quō, ut dīcunt, templum Iovis Capitōlīnī conditum est. Postquam Tarquinius Prīscus necātus est, Servius Tullius rēx est factus. Multa et ūtilia cīvibus Rōmānīs ab hōc rēge īnstitūta sunt et pāx cum populīs vīcīnīs facta est. Sed ubi Tullius ā fīliā suā crūdēlissimē necātus est, Tarquinius Superbus, cuius uxor erat Tulliī fīlia, rēgnum occupāvit. Hic Tarquinius erat septimus Rōmānōrum rēx et ultimus. Ipse enim nōmine et nātūrā superbus ā Rōmānīs expulsus est. Tum prīmum duo cōnsulēs creātī sunt."

Dum puerī cum Eucleide domum proficīscēbantur, dē lūdō loquēbantur.

"Audīvistīne tū dē rēgibus Rōmānīs, Sexte?" inquit Mārcus.

"Certē! Fābulae ā grammaticō dē rēgibus nārrātae mihi maximē placuērunt." exclāmāvit Sextus. "Grammaticum audīvī atque omnia in memoriā teneō!"

"Quid dīxit grammaticus?" rogāvit Mārcus.

Sextus respondit, "Rōmulus Pompilius erat prīmus rēx ē septendecim rēgibus quī urbem regēbant. Ūndēvīgintī templa īnstituit. Tullus Hostilius fuit decimus rēx et quīnquāgintā annōs Rōmam regēbat. Tredecim rēgēs fuērunt Etruscī. Ūndecimus rēx, nōmine Ancus Prīscus, sēdecim pontēs aedificāvit. Tullius Tarquinius quartus cōnsul ā populō est factus."

Stupuērunt Mārcus et Eucleidēs.

regō, regere, rēxī, rēctus, *to rule*
rēx, rēgis, m. *king*
templum, -ī, n., *temple*
sacer, sacra, sacrum, *holy, sacred*
   rēs sacrae, *sacred institutions*
īnstituō, īnstituere, īnstituī, īnstitūtus, *to establish, arrange*
augeō, augēre, auxī, auctus, *to increase, enlarge*

Iuppiter, Iovis, m., *Jupiter*
   Juppiter Capitōlīnus, *Capitoline Jupiter*
pāx, pācis, f., *peace*
crūdēlissimē, adv., *most/very cruelly*
superbus, -a, -um, *haughty, arrogant, proud*
occupō, -āre, -āvī, -ātus, *to seize*
ultimus, -a, -um, *last*

1. Ancus Pompilius erat prīmus rēx ē septendecim rēgibus quī urbem rēxērunt.

_____ erat prīmus rēx ē _____ rēgibus quī urbem rēxērunt.

2. Rōmulus Pompilius erat secundus rēx et undēvīgintī templa īnstituit.

_____ Pompilius erat secundus rēx et _____.

3. Tullus Hostēs fuit tertius rēx et quīnquāgintā Rōmānī eum verēbantur.

Tullus _____ fuit tertius rēx et _____ eum verēbantur.

4. Ancus Mārtius, quartus rēx, sēdecim pīstrīnās aedificāvit.

Ancus _____, quartus rēx, _____ aedificāvit.

5. Servius Prīscus erat quīntus rēx et Cūriam condidit.

_____ Prīscus erat quīntus rēx et _____ condidit.

6. Tarquinius Tullius pācem cum populīs superbīs fēcit.

_____ Tullius pācem cum populīs _____ fēcit.

7. Ultimus rēx, nōmine Tullius Tarquinius, quartus cōnsul est factus ā populō Rōmānō.

Ultimus rēx, nōmine _____, _____ ā populō Rōmānō.

A LESSON FOR SEXTUS

In addition to vocabulary and the story, the activities in this chapter focus on:
1. place constructions.
2. time constructions.

Web Code: jgd-0012

Vocabulary

Activity 39a Vocabulary

Study the vocabulary list on pages 212–214 alone or with a partner. Go to the corresponding list on the Companion website where you will find sample place and time constructions.

The Story

Activity 39b Vocabulary in Context

Fill in the blanks with Latin words to match the English cues:

1. _____ grammaticō _____. (It is important) (to obey)

2. _____ ad Hesperiam advēnērunt, Aenēās et _____ multōs annōs errābant. (Before) (companions)

3. "Conticuēre" est _____ _____ "conticuērunt." (word) (the same as)

4. Saepe poētae _____ verbum scrībunt. (thus)

5. _____ ā _____, Aenēās _____ morātus est, sed ad Hesperiam nāvigābat. (Warned) (gods) (nowhere)

6. Sextus dormitābat et grammaticus ubi eum _____,

   "_____," inquit, "manum, Sexte!" (noticed) (Hold out)

Building the Meaning

Place Constructions with and without Prepositions

Activity 39c To, From, or Already There?

Read each of the following sentences and write translations of the italicized words:

1. Cornēliī vīllam rūsticam *Baiīs* habent. _____

2. Aestāte *Baiās* iter facere solent. _____

3. Cornēliī ante fīnem aestātis *Baiīs* profectī *domum* rediērunt. _____

   _____

4. Eucleidēs līberōs *domī* cūrāre solet. _____

5. Eucleidēs puerōs cotīdiē *domō* ēdūcit quod ubi *Rōmae* sunt necesse est eīs ad lūdum īre. _____

   _____

6. Aenēās *Troiae* multōs annōs habitābat. _____

7. Aenēās *Troiā* cum comitibus iter fēcit. _____

8. Aenēās *Troiam* numquam rediit. _____

9. Aenēās *Dēlum* nāvigāvit. _____

10. Aenēās *Dēlī* breve modo tempus morātus est. _____

11. Aenēās *Dēlō* brevī tempore profectus est. _____

12. Aenēās *ā Siciliā* profectus *ad Āfricam* tempestāte āctus est. _____

    _____

13. Aenēās *Carthāginem* sextā hōrā pervēnit. _____

14. Aenēās ā Dīdōne, rēgīnā pulchrā, *Carthāginī* acceptus est. _____

15. Aenēae tamen *Carthāgine* prīmā lūce nāvigāre necesse est. _____

16. Aenēās *ab Āfricā* profectus *ad Italiam* nāvigāvit. _____

    _____

17. Aenēās Troiam novam *in Italiā* condere volēbat. _____

18. Cornēliī *rūre* rediērunt. _____

19. Cornēliī *rūs* iērunt. _____

20. Cornēliī *rūrī* sunt. _____

Activity 39d Place Constructions without Prepositions

In the second sentence in each set below, replace the italicized phrase in the first sentence with the correct form of the word in parentheses:

1. Cornēliī *ab vīllā* discēdere parant.

Cornēliī _____ discēdere parant. (**Baiae, -ārum,** f. pl.)

2. Cornēlia *ad vīllam* redīre vult.

Cornēlia _____ redīre vult. (**Baiae**)

3. Flāvia *in oppidō* habitābat.

Flāvia _____ habitābat. (**Baiae**)

4. Cornēlius *ad urbem* revocātus erat.

Cornēlius _____ revocātus erat. (**Rōma, -ae,** f.)

5. Cornēlius, dum *in Cūriā* morātur, ā prīncipe cōnsultus est.

Cornēlius, dum _____ morātur, ā prīncipe cōnsultus est. (**Rōma**)

6. Aenēās cum Dīdōne *in Āfricā* morārī volēbat.

Aenēās cum Dīdōne _____ morārī volēbat. (**Carthāgō, Carthāginis,** f.)

7. Comitēs Aenēae *ab Āfricā* nāvigāre volēbant.

Comitēs Aenēae _____ nāvigāre volēbant. (**Carthāgō**)

8. Hannibal cum patre *ad Hispāniam* iit.

Hannibal cum patre _____ iit. (**Gādēs, Gādium,** f. pl.)

9. Hannibal *ex Hispāniā* cum mīlitibus discessit.

Hannibal _____ cum mīlitibus discessit. (**Gādēs**)

10. Hannibal in *Āfricā* nōn relictus erat.

Hannibal _____ nōn relictus erat. (**domus, -ūs**, f.)

11. Cornēlius *Rōmam* iit.

Cornēlius _____ iit. (**domus**)

12. Cornēlius *Rōmā* profectus est.

Cornēlius _____ profectus est. (**domus**)

13. Flāvia in *vīllā rūsticā* manēbat.

Flāvia _____ manēbat. (**rūs, rūris**, n.)

14. Cornēlia ā *vīllā rūsticā* progressa est.

Cornēlia _____ progressa est. (**rūs**)

15. Cornēlia ad *vīllam rūsticam* mox redībit.

Cornēlia _____ mox redībit. (**rūs**)

Time Constructions with and without Prepositions

Activity 39e When or for How Long?

Circle the appropriate Latin word or phrase for the italicized English expression in each sentence below:

1. Cornēliī Rōmae *for many years* habitābant.
multīs annīs   multōs annōs   multī annī

2. Abhinc *three months* ē Bīthȳniā ēgressus sum.
tribus mēnsibus   trēs mēnsēs   trium mēnsum

3. Cornēliī *in a few months* ad vīllam rūsticam redībunt.
paucōs mēnsēs   paucī mēnsēs   paucīs mēnsibus

4. Illī canēs *for the whole night* in viīs lātrābant.
tōtam noctem   tōtā nocte   tōtīs noctibus

5. Prīnceps lūdōs circēnsēs *for four days* fēcit.
quartō diē   quattuor diēbus   quattuor diēs

6. Cornēlius ad Forum *at the second hour* profectus est.
secundam hōram   secundā hōrā   duās hōrās

7. Nāvēs Aenēae *for many days* hūc illūc āctae sunt.
   multōs diēs   multīs diēbus   multī diēs

8. Vergilius, poēta praeclārus, *in his 50th year* mortuus est.
   quīnquāgintā annōs   quīnquāgēsimō annō   quīnquāgēsimum annum

9. Aenēās ab Asiā *a few years before* vēnerat.
   paucōs annōs antequam   paucīs annīs   paucīs ante annīs

10. Aenēās *in three years* ad Italiam nāvigābit.
    trēs annī   tribus annīs   trēs annōs

11. Vergilius, *when he was eight years old*, Cremōnam missus est.
    octō annōs nātus   octō annīs   octō annīs nātus

12. *At that time* urbs Troia ā Graecīs obsidēbātur.
    ea tempora   eō tempore   id tempus

Applying What You Have Learned

Activity 39f Writing the Language

Translate the following English sentences into Latin. Include all long marks. Use the stories and vocabulary lists in your textbook, as well as the vocabulary lists in this book, to help you:

1. After one student finished reciting, another spoke in this way.

   _____

   _____

2. "Aeneas, having set out from Troy, was wandering for many years: he went to Thrace, then to Delos, then to Crete, (and) at length to Sicily.

   _____

   _____

3. "A very great storm drove Aeneas (**Aenēān**) to Carthage.

   _____

   _____

4. "Aeneas, captured by love, was delaying there for many months, and his companions were becoming very unhappy.

_____

_____

5. "In the middle of the night, however, Aeneas was warned by the gods and set out toward Italy at first light."

_____

_____

Activity 39g Expanding Your English Vocabulary

For each italicized English word below, give the related Latin word and below it the meaning of that Latin word. Then complete each sentence by filling in a word at the right:

Latin Word
Meaning of the Latin Word   **If you …**

1. _____   *monitor* a student's progress,
                                     you _____ the student regularly.   _____

_____

2. _____   *deify* the emperor, you
                                     elevate him to the status of a   _____

3. _____   have a *premonition* about
                                     an upcoming event, you have a
                                     _____ of what will happen.   _____

_____

4. _____   *verbalize* your feelings,
                                     you express them in   _____

_____

5. _____   *admonish* someone, you
                                     give a stern _____ to the person.   _____

_____

6. _____   take a *trans*-continental trip,
                                     you travel _____ the continent.   _____

_____

7. _____ visit a *mortuary*, you go to a place
_____ where _____ bodies are stored. _____

8. _____ live on a *rural* estate, your
_____ estate is located in the _____

9. _____ provide a *literal* translation
_____ of a text, you give the actual
meaning of each of its _____

10. _____ visit a neo*natal* ward, you
see babies who have just been _____

11. _____ are punished by *expulsion*
_____ you are _____ of school. _____

12. _____ have *vivid* memories, you have
_____ memories that seem to be _____

13. _____ have a *vivacious* personality, you
_____ have a personality that is full of _____

14. _____ *migrate* from one city to
another, you _____ your home. _____
_____

Activity 39h Reading Latin

Look at the new vocabulary following this story. Then read the story, noting expressions of time and place and forms of **domus** *and* **rūs**. *Reread the story for comprehension. Then mark whether each statement about the story is* **V = Vērum** *(True) or* **F = Falsum** *(False):*

Sextus Prepares to Pay the Penalty

Sextus extrā lūdum stābat sōlus. Miser ac sollicitus sēcum cōgitābat, "Quid

iam faciam? Quid faciet Eucleidēs? Quid Cornēliō dīcet?" Puer miser horruit.

"Certē Rōmā discēdam et Baiās redībō nam īre Pompeiōs, ubi nātus sum, nōn

possum quod illud oppidum dēlētum est. Baiīs rūrī habitāre volō. Ūsque ad

Sīciliam īre possum! Carthāginem migrāre possum! Fortasse in Italiā manēbō et

Cremōnae vel Mediolānī complūrēs annōs habitābō. Etiam ad patrem trāns mare ībō."

Dum ibi stat, ē lūdō vēnit Eucleidēs. "Ignāve puer! Cūr magistrō nōn pārēs? Haec omnia Cornēliō mox nārrābuntur. Propter tē duās hōrās per urbem iter faciam, nam mihi necesse erit ad lūdum redīre et Mārcum domum redūcere." Itaque Sextus per viās urbis domum ductus est.

Ubi Cornēlius ē Forō vesperī rediit, Eucleidēs ātrium intrāvit. Cornēlius īrācundus quod dēfessus erat, "Quid est?" inquit.

"Dē Sextō rem atrōcem tibi nārrāre volō," respondit Eucleidēs.

Cui Cornēlius cum gemitū, "Ō mē miserum!" inquit. "Quid iam fēcit Sextus?"

"Hodiē grammaticus, īrātus quod Sextus labōrāre nōlēbat, eum ē lūdō expulit. Eum redīre vetuit."

"Quid?" exclāmāvit Cornēlius. "Sextus ē lūdō expulsus est? Dūc eum statim ad mē!"

Intereā Sextus sollicitus in lectō iacēbat et sēcum cōgitābat, "Quid mihi dīcet Cornēlius? Iam Rōmae cum Cornēliō manēre nōlō, sed in Asiā cum patre habitāre volō." Eō ipsō tempore intrāvit Eucleidēs.

"Age!" inquit. "Surge! Cornēlius tibi pauca dīcere vult."

Gemuit Sextus et "Aegrōtō," inquit. "Surgere nōn possum."

"Fabulās! Verēris, nōn aegrōtās. Surge statim! Tempus est poenās dare."

Invītus tandem Sextus surrēxit atque in ātrium ab Eucleide ductus est. Tremēbat neque Cornēlium spectāre volēbat. Ō miserum Sextum!

horreō, horrēre, horruī, *to shudder*
ūsque, adv., *all the way*
īrācundus, -a, -um, *irritable, in a bad mood*
atrōx, atrōcis, *horrible, atrocious*
gemitus, -ūs, m., *groan, sigh*
poenās dare, *to pay the penalty, be punished*

1. Sextus ē ludō expulsus Baiās et rūs redīre nōluit.   V   F

2. Sextus Cremōnā expulsus Pompēiōs redīre voluit.   V   F

3. Sextus fortasse Carthāginī aut in Siciliā habitābit.   V   F

4. Sextus duās hōrās Eucleidem exspectābat.   V   F

5. Eucleidēs Sextum invītum domō trāxit.   V   F

6. Eucleidēs cum Cornēliō dē Sextō domī locūtus est.   V   F

7. Sextus rūrī cum patre suō habitāre voluit.   V   F

8. Sextus cum Cornēliō loquī potuit quod nōn aegrōtābat.   V   F

Name _____ Date _____ Period _____

TO FATHER FROM SEXTUS

In addition to vocabulary and the story, the activities in this chapter focus on:
1. semi-deponent verbs.
2. present participles and participial phrases.
3. alternative translations of participial phrases.
4. present participles as substantives.

Go Online
PHSchool.com
Web Code: jgd-0013

Vocabulary

Activity 40a Vocabulary

Study the vocabulary listed at the back of this book alone or with a partner.

The Story

Activity 40b Vocabulary in Context

Fill in the blanks with Latin words to match the English cues:

1. Sextus scrīpsit, "Sī _____, mī pater, ego gaudeō!" (you are well)

2. _____ Sextus rūrī laetus habitābat quod in marī _____

   poterat. (At first) (to swim)

3. _____ regressus arborēs ascendēbat et ex eīs _____.
   (From there) (he used to jump down)

4. Sextus ignāvus nōn erat. _____ lupum _____

   _____. (On the contrary) (to drive off) (he dared)

5. In lūdō semper erat miser, _____ grammaticum _____
   habēret. (since) (most cruel)

6. Sextus semper _____ _____ sed,

   _____ respondēre cōnātus est, grammaticus ferulam

   _____ et eum verberābat! (to learn) (was desiring) (as soon as) (used to seize)

7. Sextus semper _____. (was being punished)

8. Cēterī discipulī quoque _____ ubi esset Hesperia. (were ignorant of)

9. Sextus scrīpsit, "_____ mē miserrimum, pater, _____,

_____." (Send for) (I beg) (as soon as possible)

Forms

Semi-deponent Verbs

Activity 40c Semi-deponent Verbs in Context

Fill in the blanks to match the English cues. Note subjects carefully before you decide what form of the verb to use:

1. Sextus _____ quod in marī natāre eī licuit. (was glad)

2. Quamquam Eucleidēs Baiīs adfuerat, ad lītus īre nōn _____.
(had been accustomed)

3. Eucleidēs, dum Rōmae habitat, cotīdiē in Argīlētō errāre _____.
(is accustomed)

4. Līberī in silvīs errāre _____. (were accustomed)

5. Puellae lupum ingentem repellere nōn _____. (did dare)

6. "_____! Lupus ē silvā expulsus est." (Rejoice – pl.)

7. "Certē _____, Cornēlia, ubi lupus expulsus est." (you rejoiced)

8. "_____ quod ille lupus in hanc silvam redīre nōn _____."
(I am glad) (will dare)

9. Eucleidēs, postquam praedōnēs eum in Subūrā ambulantem petere _____,

eō īre nōn _____. (dared) (did dare).

10. Propter īrācundiam Palaemonis, Sextus vix ad lūdum īre _____. (dared)

Building the Meaning

Present Participles

Activity 40d Participial Phrases

Complete the following sentences with participles, keeping to the English cues. Make the participles agree in gender, case, and number with the italicized words. Underline all participial phrases.

1. *Sextus* Baiīs _____ ad lītus saepe ībat. (living/dwelling)

2. *Sextus* magnā vōce _____ *Dāvum* in hortō _____ saepe vexābat. (shouting) (working)

3. Lupus *puerīs* in silvā _____ appropinquāvit. (walking)

4. Vōx *Mārcī* lupum _____ ā Cornēliā audīta est. (driving away)

5. Deinde Cornēlia *Mārcum* magnō rāmō lupum _____ vīdit. (driving away)

6. Sextus nūllum auxilium *Mārcō* lupum _____ tulit. (driving away)

7. *Cornēliīs* iter Rōmam _____ magnum malum accidit. (making)

Activity 40e Alternative Translations of Participial Phrases

Participial phrases can be translated using relative clauses or clauses introduced by as, when, while, because, since, *or* although. *Use such a clause in your translation of each of the sentences below, making sure that it is in keeping with the meaning of the sentence as a whole and that the tense of its verb is appropriate. Underline all participial phrases:*

1. Palaemōn Sextum semper discere cupientem saepe verberat.

_____

_____

2. Sextus Palaemōnī difficillima rogantī respondēre nōn poterat.

_____

_____

3. Cēterī puerī dē Hesperiā scientēs rēctē respondēre potuērunt.

_____

_____

4. Aenēās ipse ignōrāns ubi esset Hesperia ad Āfricam errāvit.

_____

_____

5. Magister Sextum dē Hesperiā ignōrantem crūdēlissimē verberāvit.

_____

_____

6. Sextus domum intrāns ā Cornēliō arcessītus est.

_____

_____

7. Cornēlius Sextum rem explicāre cōnantem iterum pūnīvit.

_____

_____

8. Sextus miserē aegrōtāns epistulam ad patrem mittit.

_____

_____

Present Participles as Substantives

Activity 40f Participles as Substantives

Replace the underlined words in the first of each of the sentences below with a participle used as a substantive in the second sentence. Then translate the second sentence:

1. Heri erant tempestātēs perīculōsae <u>eīs quī nāvigābant</u>.

Heri erant tempestātēs perīculōsae _____.

_____

2. Hodiē clāmōrēs <u>eōrum quī natant</u> audīre potestis.

Hodiē clāmōrēs _____ audīre potestis.

_____

3. In Amphitheātrō <u>virōs quī pugnant</u> vidēmus.

In Amphitheātrō _____ vidēmus.

_____

4. Nōnnumquam clāmōrēs <u>eōrum quī moriuntur</u> audiuntur.

Nōnnumquam clāmōrēs _____ audiuntur.

_____

5. Expergīsciminī, <u>vōs quī dormītis</u>!

Expergīsciminī, _____!

_____

Applying What You Have Learned

Activity 40g Writing the Language

Translate the following English sentences into Latin. Include all long marks. Use the stories and vocabulary lists in your textbook, as well as the vocabulary lists in this book, to help you:

1. At Baiae Sextus used to watch the boats approaching the shore.

_____

2. Marcus, when he was sitting in a tree (use present participle), caught sight of two wolves attacking the girls.

_____

3. Sextus, because he was learning nothing in school (use **quod** clause), was often beaten on account of the bad temper of the teacher, Palaemon.

_____

_____

4. Palaemon was always in the habit of asking Sextus very difficult things.

_____

5. Today Sextus did not rejoice when Palaemon asked him about Hesperia.

_____

Activity 40h Expanding Your English Vocabulary

Using the word bank below, write the word that could replace the italicized word or words in each sentence. Use the Latin words in parentheses to help determine the meaning of the English words. Then write the English translation of each Latin word in the word bank:

1. Sextus wrote to his father that it was he who *drove off* the wolf. _____

2. Sextus ended his letter with the typical *goodbye*. _____

3. Sextus had the *boldness* to claim that he had saved the girls. _____

4. Sextus was trying to present a *well-grounded* argument to his father. _____

5. Sextus hoped his father would be unable to *test the truth of* his stories. _____

6. Sextus *disregarded* the real facts when he wrote his letter. _____

7. Sextus's father could not immediately determine the *truth* of his son's claims. _____

8. To Palaemon, Sextus seems to be an *ignorant person*. _____

9. Under Roman law, engaging in piracy was a *legally punishable* offense. _____

10. Pseudolus was punished for his *greed*. _____

11. Cornelia was in a state of *ecstasy* at her first visit to the Circus Maximus. _____

penal **(poena)** _____	repelled **(repellere)** _____
rapture **(rapere)** _____	cupidity **(cupere)** _____
valediction **(valēre)** _____	audacity **(audēre)** _____
verify **(vērus)** _____	valid **(valēre)** _____
ignored **(ignōrāre)** _____	veracity **(vērus)** _____
ignoramus **(ignōrāre)** _____	

Activity 40i Reading Latin

Look at the new vocabulary following this story. Then read the Latin of the story, noting semi-deponent verbs and present participles. Reread the Latin for comprehension. Then match the first part of each sentence that follows to the phrase or clause that correctly completes it:

An Outing

Mārcus et Sextus in ātriō sedēbant cum subitō Titus patruus in ātrium ab iānitōre dēductus est. Ille ingrediēns magnō cum gaudiō ā puerīs salūtātus est, nam diū āfuerat.

"Quid agis?" simul clāmāvērunt.

"Aquam Marciam mihi statim vīsitāre necesse est. Caesar mē servōs aquaeductum cūrantēs monēre vult. Cīvēs quīdam aquae cōpiam fūrantur et ad vīllās et fundōs dēvertunt. Vultisne mēcum īre?"

Puerī cum gaudiō saluērunt. Cornēlius enim eōs sōlōs exīre nōn sinēbat, sed cum Titō forās īre eīs licēbat. Ille puerōs ad lectīcās iam conductās et lectīcāriōs expectantēs dūxit.

Celeriter per viās urbis Titum et puerōs ferēbant lectīcāriī. Tandem haud longē ā Portā Capēnā aberant et arcūs magnōs aquaeductūs suprā urbem exstantēs vidēre poterant. Mox magnam turbam servōrum dīligenter labōrantium cōnspexērunt. Aliī arcūs rīmōsōs summā dīligentiā reficiēbant, aliī lapidēs quadrātōs summīs vīribus movēbant. Undique clāmor et strepitus.

Tum Titus servum quendam, hominem Graecum, vīdit et agnōvit. Titus stupuit. Puerī rīsērunt. Ille, homō obēsus et īgnāvus, humī iacēbat vehementer stertēns, nam diēs calidus erat. Titus īrā commōtus hominem miserum excitāvit et reprehendit. Ille, ē somnō vix excitātus, attonitus surrēxit et Titum, cūrātōrem aquārum, salūtāvit.

Titus tamen neque īrācundus neque malevolus esse solēbat. Postquam eum trementem paulisper spectāvit, rīsit et magnā vōce clāmāvit, "Servōsne iubēbō lectum tuum hūc adferre? Mehercule! Sī forte hic aquaeductus ad terram cadet, tū certē fragōrem nōn audiēs! Nōn sine causā Caesar est sollicitus."

dēdūcō, dēdūcere, dēdūxī, dēductus, *to show into, bring, escort*
cōpia, -ae, f., *large quantity*
fūror, -ārī, -ātus sum, *to steal, pilfer*
fundus, -ī, m., *farm*
saliō, salīre, saluī, saltūrus, *to jump*
forās, adv., *outside*
haud, adv., *not*
vīrēs, vīrium, f. pl., *strength*
cūrātor, cūrātōris, m., *overseer, superintendent*
malevolus, -a, -um, *ill-disposed*

1. Titus ātrium ingressus est in quō . . . _____

2. Caesar voluit Titum monēre servōs quī . . . _____

3. Titus et puerī appropinquāvērunt lectīcīs conductīs

et . . . _____

4. Puerī haud longē ā Portā Capēnā vīdērunt

aquaeductum . . . _____

5. Puerī cōnspexērunt servōs quōsdam . . . _____

6. Puerī cōnspexērunt aliōs quoque servōs . . . _____

7. Vehementer stertēbat homō īgnāvus quī . . . _____

a. aquaeductum cūrābant.

b. arcūs rīmōsōs dīligentissimē

reficientēs.

c. humī iacēbat.

d. lapidēs quadrātōs moventēs.

e. lectīcāriīs exspectantibus.

f. Mārcus et Sextus sedēbant.

g. suprā urbem exstantem.

DRAMATIC NEWS

Go Online
PHSchool.com
Web Code: jgd-0014

In addition to vocabulary and the story, the activities in this chapter focus on:
1. perfect active infinitives.
2. participial phrases (review).

Activity 41a **Vocabulary**

Study the vocabulary list on page 216 alone or with a partner.

The Story

Activity 41b **Vocabulary in Context**

Fill in the blanks with Latin words to match the English cues:

1. Cornēlia tēlam multās hōrās _____. (had woven)

2. Nōn licēbat eī cum puerīs _____ _____. (to go outside)

3. Verba servī _____ audiēbat. (with much enthusiasm)

4. Eam _____ audīre dēlectābat. (such things)

5. "_____ tē dēlectābit," inquit Aurēlia, "Valerium vidēre!" (How much…!)

6. Valerius _____ Brundisiō abhinc trēs diēs discessisse. (is said)

Forms

Verbs: Perfect Active Infinitive

41c **Perfect Active Infinitives**

Using the third principal parts listed below, form and translate the perfect active infinitives of these verbs:

1. intrāvī _____ _____

2. comparāvī _____ _____

3. sēdī _____ _____

4. texuī _____ _____

5. cupīvī _____ _____

6. sepelīvī _____ _____

7. fuī _____ _____

8. voluī _____ _____

9. noluī _____ _____

10. tulī _____ _____

Review

Participial Phrases

Activity 41d Participial Phrases

Underline any participles in the Latin sentences and draw lines from them to the nouns that they modify. Then, translate the sentences into English:

1. Flāvia cum Cornēliā Rōmam regrediente īre nōn poterat.

_____

_____

2. Flāvia sōla in cubiculō sedēns dē amīcā suā optimā cōgitābat.

_____

_____

3. "Quandō," sēcum cōgitābat, "Cornēliam rūrsus vidēbō?"

_____

_____

4. "Quantum eam dēsīderō!"

_____

5. Eō ipsō tempore patrem cum mātre in ātriō loquentem audīvit.

_____

_____

6. Flāvia quam celerrimē ē cubiculō ēgressa in ātrium intrāvit.

_____

_____

7. Cum prīmum parentēs cōnspexit, "Pater māterque," inquit, "Baiīs diūtius morātī sumus. Licetne nōbīs Rōmam īre?"

_____

_____

8. Pater Flāviae rogantī respondit: "Fortasse, parvula. Epistulam ad Cornēlium mittam."

_____

_____

9. "Sī ille nōs invītāverit, illūc ībimus."

_____

Applying What You Have Learned

Activity 41e Writing the Language

Translate the following English sentences into Latin. Include all long marks. Use the stories and vocabulary lists in your textbook, as well as the vocabulary lists in this book, to help you:

1. Aurelia said, "Valerius is said to have been away in Bithynia for several months."

_____

_____

2. "He is said, however, to have arrived in Italy five days ago."

_____

_____

3. The slave said, "My master, Valerius, is said to have departed from the inn three days ago."

_____

_____

4. Cornelia said to her mother, "How much it delights me to have heard about Valerius!

_____

_____

5. "He is said to have escaped from many dangers."

_____

_____

Activity 41f Expanding Your English Vocabulary

For each italicized English word below, give the related Latin word and below it the meaning of that Latin word. Then complete each sentence by filling in a word at the right:

Latin Word
Meaning of the Latin Word

If you …

1. _____   are a *foreigner*, you come
                                      from a place that lies
_____   _____ the borders of the   _____
                                      country where you are now.

2. _____ are a *studious* member of
   the class, you prepare for
   _____ each class with diligence and _____

3. _____ are a *textile* merchant,
   you sell cloth that has been
   _____ _____

4. _____ are measuring the *quantity* of
   something, you are trying to
   _____ determine _____ of it there is. _____

Activity 41g Reading Latin

Look at the new vocabulary following this story. Then read the story, noting the perfect active infinitives. Reread the story for comprehension. Then answer the questions with complete Latin sentences.

Who Is Valerius?

Cornēlia Flāviae cārissimae S.P.D.

Avē, mea amīca. Quantum tē dēsīderō! Quantum haec urbs mihi nōn placet!

Cotīdiē tēlam sōla texēns domī sine amīcīs sedeō. Mārcus Sextusque, illī puerī

fēlīcissimī, forās eunt ad lūdum ubi semper sunt aliī puerī. Sextus tamen nihil

in lūdō discere vidētur, nam sine studiō eō īre solet. Grammaticus quidem

saepissimē vexāvisse dīcitur. Quod ē lūdō ā grammaticō, virō īrātissimō, ēiectus

erat, pater meus īrācundus puerum graviter pūnīvisse dīcitur. Trēs diēs ille

mēcum domī morātus est. Haud multum hoc mihi placēbat, nam Sextus molestus

semper est. Iam, postquam poenās dedit, ad lūdum cum Mārcō rediit.

Noster Eucleidēs ā praedōnibus scelestīs petītus est et pecūnia ab eō ērepta

est. Sōlus per Subūram, partem urbis perīculōsissimam, ambulābat et dīcitur in

lutō graviter vulnerātus diū iacuisse. Ō miserum servum!

Hodiē tamen aliquid novī! Servus Quīntī Valeriī advēnit et mihi mātrīque

nova dē dominō suō dīxit. Ā nōbīs audīta est fābula optima dē Valeriō, virō

fortissimō, nārrāta, quī Rōmam ā Bīthȳniā regrediēns perīcula dolōremque passus est. Quīntus Valerius est adulēscēns nōbilis, cuius pater est vir praeclārus et patrī meō nōtissimus. Valerius dīcitur tribūnus legiōnis in Germaniā abhinc paucōs annōs fuisse. Nūper Valerius et pater eius cum praetōre Bīthȳniae fuērunt et Valerius dīcitur aquaeductūs et aedificia pūblica ibi cūrāvisse. Tālibus officiīs, ut pater dīcit, funguntur adulēscentēs quī rem pūblicam capessere volunt.

Iam māter paterque multa dē Valeriō mē saepius rogant: "Placetne ille tibi, Cornēlia? Vīsne Quīntum Valerium rūrsus vidēre?" Certē est adulēscēns optimus quī mihi placet et quem rūrsus vidēre volō. Tē quoque rūrsus vidēre volō, mea Flāvia. Sī Rōmam ad mē vēneris, tū quoque Quīntum Valerium nōveris. Valē!

> **haud**, adv., *not*
> **tribūnus, -ī**, m., *tribune*
> > **tribūnus legiōnis**, *military tribune (a military officer)*
> **nūper**, adv., *recently*
> **praetor, praetōris**, m., *praetor, governor*
> **officium, -ī**, n., *official engagement, business, duty*
> **fungor, fungī, fūnctus sum** + abl., *to perform*
> **capessō, capessere, capessīvī**, *to take up, engage in*
> > **rem pūblicam capessere**, *to engage in public life or politics*
> **nōveris**, *you will get to know*

1. Quis dīcitur Sextum ē lūdō ēiēcisse?

_____

2. Quis dīcitur cum Cornēliā domī paulisper mānsisse?

_____

3. Quis dīcitur sōlus per perīculōsam partem urbis ambulāvisse?

_____

4. Quī dīcuntur pecūniam ab Eucleide ēripuisse?

_____

5. Quid servus Quīntī Valeriī dīcitur Cornēliae Aurēliaeque nārrāvisse?

_____

6. Quis dīcitur in Bīthȳniā nūper fuisse?

_____

7. Quī dīcuntur Cornēliam multa dē adulēscente rogāvisse?

_____

A Slave to the Rescue

In addition to vocabulary and the story, the activities in this chapter focus on:

1. the imperfect and pluperfect subjunctive active.
2. subordinate clauses with the subjunctive: **cum** causal, **cum** circumstantial, and indirect questions.
3. identifying **cum** clauses as *circumstantial* or *causal*, and translating accordingly.
4. identifying the direct question reported in an indirect question.

Go Online
PHSchool.com
Web Code: jgd-0015

Vocabulary

Activity 42a Vocabulary

Study the vocabulary list on page 217 alone or with a partner.

The Story

Activity 42b Vocabulary in Context

Fill in the blanks with Latin words to match the English cues:

1. Nāvis _____ ad īnsulam quandam ācta est. (by the wind)

2. Cum pīrātae nāvem _____, _____ eīs

   _____ nōlēbat. (attacked) (the captain) (to resist)

3. "Sumus omnēs," inquit, "_____, sed hic Rōmānus _____
   est." (poor) (rich)

4. _____ omnēs dormīrent, servus _____ īre poterat ad

   _____ ubi pīrātae Valerium custōdiēbant. (Since) (secretly) (hut)

5. Servus duōs custōdēs _____. (overcame)

6. Itaque Valerius et servus in scaphā _____. (escaped)

7. In scaphā per _____ diū nāvigāvērunt. (waves)

Forms

Verbs: Imperfect and Pluperfect Subjunctives

Activity 42c Forming Imperfect and Pluperfect Subjunctives

Give the imperfect and pluperfect subjunctive active in the 3rd person singular of the following verbs:

	Imperfect Subjunctive	Pluperfect Subjunctive
1. obsideō, obsidēre, obsēdī	_____	_____
2. dēleō, dēlēre, dēlēvī	_____	_____
3. percutiō, percutere, percussī	_____	_____
4. adimō, adimere, adēmī	_____	_____
5. dēsiliō, dēsilīre, dēsiluī	_____	_____
6. discō, discere, didicī	_____	_____
7. condō, condere, condidī	_____	_____
8. poscō, poscere, poposcī	_____	_____
9. iaciō, iacere, iēcī	_____	_____
10. compleō, complēre, complēvī	_____	_____

Building the Meaning

Subordinate Clauses with the Subjunctive II

Activity 42d Recognizing Subjunctive Verbs in Subordinate Clauses

Below are two pairs of very similar sentences. One sentence has a subordinate clause with an indicative verb, the other a subordinate clause with a subjunctive verb. First underline the verb in each subordinate clause. Then in the blank provided identify whether the verb is indicative or subjunctive, and identify its tense:

1a. Proximō diē, cum ab īnsulā nāvigārēmus, complūrēs scaphās hominum plēnās cōnspeximus.

_____   _____

1b. Proximō diē, ubi ab īnsulā nāvigābāmus, complūrēs scaphās hominum plēnās cōnspeximus.

_____   _____

2a. Quoniam multōs diēs in scaphā fuerant, Valerius et servus graviter aegrōtābant.

_____ _____

2b. Cum multōs diēs in scaphā fuissent, Valerius et servus graviter aegrōtābant.

_____ _____

Activity 42e Identifying *cum* Clauses as Circumstantial or Causal

Based on the sense of the sentence, decide whether the **cum** *clause is circumstantial (when) or causal (since) and write your answer in the blank provided. Then translate each sentence into English:*

1. Cum complūrēs scaphās hominum plēnās cōnspexissēmus, magister nostrae nāvis "Illī hominēs sunt pīrātae," exclāmāvit.

Type of **cum** clause: _____

_____

_____

2. Cum mercātōrēs eōs bene cūrāvissent, Valerius et servus convaluērunt.

Type of **cum** clause: _____

_____

_____

3. Cum Valerius iam convaluisset, Cornēlia mātrī exclāmāvit, "Quam laeta sum!"

Type of **cum** clause: _____

_____

_____

4. Valerius, cum Rōmam advēnisset, Cornēliōs statim vīsitāre volēbat.

Type of **cum** clause: _____

_____

_____

Activity 42f Identifying the Direct Question Reported in an Indirect Question

In each sentence below, insert the verb that correctly completes the indirect question. Then translate the sentence. Finally, write in English what the direct question would have been that is stated here indirectly:

1. Illī mercātōrēs Valerium rogāvērunt quō iter _____.

    facit   faciēbat   faceret

_____

_____

2. Aurēlia petīvit unde servus iter _____.

    faciunt   fēcisset   fēcit

_____

_____

3. Pīrātae rogāvērunt quis dīves _____.

    esset   erat   fuit

_____

_____

4. Servus sē rogābat ubi pīrātae dominum _____.

    custōdīvissent   custōdīverant   custōdīrent

_____

_____

5. Aurēlia servum rogāvit cūr Valerius Rōmam nōndum _____.

    advenit   advēnit   advēnisset

_____

_____

6. Cornēlia quaesīvit quandō Valerius Brundisiō _____.

    discedet   discessisset   discessit

_____

_____

Applying What You Have Learned

Activity 42g Writing the Language

Translate the following English sentences into Latin. Include all long marks. Use the stories and vocabulary lists in your textbook, as well as the vocabulary lists in this book, to help you:

1. When Valerius was sailing from Bithynia to Rome, his ship was driven by the winds and waves to a certain island.

_____

_____

2. Since the storm was so great, they delayed a whole night on the shore.

_____

_____

3. At dawn, when they were sailing again, they suddenly saw small boats filled with men.

_____

_____

4. The captain, when he had seen the pirates, exclaimed, "We will not escape! We cannot resist them!"

_____

_____

5. Valerius, when he tried to attack the pirates, was wounded.

_____

_____

6. Since Valerius had received a serious wound, his slave also jumped into the pirates' small boat.

_____

_____

Activity 42h Expanding Your English Vocabulary

Using the word bank below, write the word that could replace the italicized word or words in each sentence. Use the Latin words in parentheses to help determine the meaning of the English words. Then write the English translation of each Latin word in the word bank:

1. Valerius and his slave managed to *escape from* the pirates. _____

2. Roman houses were designed to provide a great deal of *air flow*. _____

3. The ship's captain thought that any *opposition* to the pirates would be useless. _____

4. In dealing with the pirates, Valerius tried to pretend he was a *poor person*. _____

5. The *wave-like* motion of the dancer's arms kept her audience fascinated. _____

6. Valerius's response to the pirates was *intentionally vague*. _____

7. After being wounded, Valerius needed several days in Brundisium for *recovering his health*. _____

8. In order to combat *the condition of being poor*, free wheat was distributed to the people of ancient Rome. _____

pauper (**pauper**) _____	convalescence (**convalēscere**)
evasive (**ēvādere**) _____	_____
poverty (**pauper**) _____	undulating (**unda**) _____
resistance (**resistere**) _____	ventilation (**ventus**) _____
	evade (**ēvādere**) _____

Activity 42i Reading Latin

Look at the new vocabulary beneath this story. Then read the Latin of the story, noting imperfect and pluperfect subjunctives in **cum** *clauses and indirect questions. Reread the Latin for comprehension. Then correct the statements about the story that follow by rewriting the sentences:*

Pirates

Cum Cornēlia et Aurēlia fābulam dē Valeriō pīrātīsque nārrātam audīvissent, servus Valeriī ad domum suam rediit. Aurēlia et Cornēlia inter sē dē Valeriō paulisper loquēbantur. Cum puerōs ā lūdō redeuntēs audīrent, Cornēlia clāmāvit, "Mārce! Sexte! Hūc celerrimē venīte et audīte aliquid novī!"

Brevī tempore puerī aderant. "Quid novī est, Cornēlia? Habēsne novam pūpam?" Sextus cum rīsū rogāvit.

"Tacē, moleste!" respondit Cornēlia. "Fābulam novam dē Valeriō nārrātam audīvimus!"

"Quid dē Valeriō audīvistī?" rogāvit Mārcus. "Mihi valdē placet ille adulēscēns, quī diū āfuit."

"Quis est Valerius?" rogāvit Sextus.

Aurēlia, cum Sextō explicāvisset quis esset Valerius et ubi fuisset, "Fābula dē pīrātīs perīculīsque nōbīs nārrāta est!" inquit. "Fābulam puerīs dīc, Cornēlia."

"Dīc nōbīs, dīc!" clāmāvit Sextus. "Omnia dē pīrātīs audīre volō!"

Itaque Cornēlia puerīs nārrāvit quōmodo pīrātae armātī Valerium resistentem superāvissent, quōmodo auxiliō servī fidēlis ēvāsisset adulēscēns, quī dominum servumque valdē aegrōtantēs Brundisium attulissent. "Mox Valerius ad urbem adveniet, nam iam convaluit."

Eō ipsō tempore ingressus est Cornēlius, quī omnia dē Valeriō in Forō iam audīverat. "Certē mare nostrum perīculōsum est, ut audīvistis, sed abhinc multōs annōs mare multō perīculōsius fuit. Fuērunt in marī plūrimī pīrātae quī nāvēs Rōmānās adortī sunt et cīvēs Rōmānōs captōs in servitūtem Dēlī vēndidērunt. Cum pīrātae urbēs Italiae ipsās dīripuissent, Pompeius Magnus ad eōs opprimendōs missus est, quamquam quīdam ē senātōribus tantam potestātem ūnī virō trādere nōlēbant. Brevissimō tempore Pompeius, cum nāvēs suās per omnia maria disposuisset, orbem terrārum pīrātīs līberāvit et pīrātās victōs aut in servitūtem dedit aut interfēcit."

Tacēbat Sextus, quī cōgitābat quōmodo ipse quoque pīrātīs resistere et eōs superāre posset.

pūpa, -ae, f., *doll*
servitūs, servitūtis, f., *slavery*
dīripiō, dīripere, dīripuī, dīreptus, *to ravage, pillage*
ad eōs opprimendōs, *to crush them*
potestās, potestātis, f., *power, authority*
dispōnō, dispōnere, disposuī, dispositus, *to place here and there, station, arrange*
orbis, orbis, m., *circle*
   orbis terrārum, *the earth, world*
līberō, -āre, -āvī, -ātus, *to set free*
interficiō, interficere, interfēcī, interfectus, *to kill*

1. Cum servī Valeriī domum pūrgāvissent, Aurēlia et Cornēlia dē Valeriō loquēbantur.

_____

_____

2. Cum puerī domum cōnspexissent, Sextus Cornēliam rogāvit quid novī esset.

_____

_____

3. Sextus, cum omnia ab Aurēliā dicta nārrāvisset, fābulam dē Valeriō nārrātam audīre voluit.

_____

_____

4. Cum plūrimī pīrātae in maribus natārent, maria perīculōsissima erant.

_____

_____

5. Cornēlius omnibus nārrāvit quōmodo Pompeius Magnus pīrātās scelestissimōs ōlim adiūvisset.

_____

_____

6. Sextus et Mārcus, cum dē pīrātīs cōgitārent, tacēbant.

_____

AT THE BATHS

In addition to vocabulary and the story, the activities in this chapter focus on:
1. imperfect and pluperfect subjunctive passive.
2. subordinate clauses with the subjunctive (review).

Vocabulary

Activity 43a Vocabulary

Study the vocabulary list on pages 218–219 alone or with a partner.

The Story

Activity 43b Vocabulary in Context

Fill in the blanks with Latin words to match the English cues:

1. Titus Cornēlius in _____ Thermārum Nerōnēārum amīcōs quōsdam exspectābat. (entrance passage)

2. _____ cum amīcī pervēnissent, omnēs in palaestram iniērunt. (There/ To that place)

3. Titus et amīcī, cum sē diū _____, in caldārium ingressī sunt. (had exercised)

4. Quod _____ et vapōrem vix patī poterant, _____ multum morātī in palaestram regressī sunt. (heat) (not)

5. Ibi vīdērunt _____ tunicā russātā _____ quī

   _____ concrepābat, dum servus pilam _____. (old man) (clothed) (fingers) (was recovering)

6. Amīcī vīnum bibentēs Titum multa rogāre coepērunt, nam omnia quae senātus

   _____ incendia ageret _____ volēbant. (against) (to find out)

Forms

Imperfect and Pluperfect Subjunctive: Active and Passive

Activity 43c Imperfect and Pluperfect Subjunctive: Active and Passive

Write the missing principal parts of **exerceō** *and* **cognōscō**. *Then give the imperfect and pluperfect subjunctives, active and passive, of these verbs in the specified persons and numbers:*

1. exerceō   _____   _____   _____

2. cognōscō   _____   _____   _____

3. 2nd sing.:   Imperfect Subjunctive: Pluperfect Subjunctive:
    (exerceō)
            Active: _____   Active: _____

            Passive: _____   Passive (masc.): _____

4. 3rd sing.:   Imperfect Subjunctive   Pluperfect Subjunctive
    (cognōscō)
            Active: _____   Active: _____

            Passive: _____   Passive (neut.): _____

Building the Meaning

Subordinate Clauses with the Subjunctive (Review)

Activity 43d *Cum* Causal Clauses

The first two sentences in each item have been joined together in the third by changing the first sentence into a **cum** *causal clause. Supply the missing subjunctives and translate the combined sentences into English:*

1. Cornēlius sē nimis exercuerat. Cornēlius maximē dēfessus erat.

   Cornēlius, cum sē nimis _____, maximē dēfessus erat.

   _____

2. Cornēlius in caldāriō calōrem vix patī poterat. Cornēlius haud multum ibi morātus est.

   Cornēlius, cum in caldāriō calōrem vix patī _____, haud multum ibi morātus est.

   _____

   _____

3. Cornēlius calōre caldāriī paene oppressus erat. Cornēlius in tepidārium regressus est.

Cornēlius, cum calōre caldāriī paene _____, in tepidārium regressus est.

_____

_____

4. Cornēlius tergērī volēbat. Cornēlius ē tepidāriō ēgressus est.

Cornēlius, cum tergērī _____, ē tepidāriō ēgressus est.

_____

5. Virī in thermīs diū collocūtī erant. Virī domum sērō discessērunt.

Virī, cum in thermīs diū _____, domum sērō discessērunt.

_____

Activity 43e *Cum* Circumstantial Clauses

The first two sentences in each item have been joined together in the third by changing the first sentence into a **cum** *circumstantial clause. Supply the missing subjunctives and translate the combined sentences into English:*

1. Cornēlius in Campum Mārtium dēscenderat. Cornēlius in Thermās Nerōnēās ingressus est.

Cornēlius, cum in Campum Mārtium _____, in Thermās Nerōnēās ingressus est.

_____

2. Cornēlius amīcīs heri occurrerat. Cornēlius amīcōs dē rēbus urbānīs rogāvit.

Cornēlius, cum amīcīs heri _____, eōs dē rēbus urbānīs rogāvit.

_____

3. Cornēlius in vestibulum ingrediēbātur. Cornēlius ab amīcīs salūtābātur.

Cornēlius, cum in vestibulum _____, ab amīcīs salūtātus est.

_____

4. Cornēlius ab amīcīs salūtātus erat. Cornēlius in apodytērium iniit.

Cornēlius, cum ab amīcīs _____, in apodytērium iniit.

_____

5. Cornēlius et amīcī in palaestram inībant. Multī cīvēs ibi sē exercēbant.

Cum Cornēlius et amīcī in palaestram _____, multī cīvēs ibi sē exercēbant.

_____

_____

6. Aliī lūctābantur. Cornēlius cum duōbus amīcīs trigōne lūdēbat.

Cum aliī _____, Cornēlius cum duōbus amīcīs trigōne lūdēbat.

_____

Activity 43f Indirect Questions

In each set below, the direct question has been transformed into an indirect question after the verb **rogābant.** *Supply the missing subjunctives, and translate the sentences into English:*

1. Quid audīvīstī dē rēbus urbānīs, Tite?

Rogābant Titum quid dē rēbus urbānīs _____.

_____

2. Quid agitur in senātū, Tite?

Rogābant Titum quid in senātū _____.

_____

3. Quid prīnceps contrā incendia facit, Tite?

Rogābant Titum quid prīnceps contrā incendia _____.

_____

4. Quī hominēs praeclārī iam in urbe adsunt, Tite?

Rogābant Titum quī hominēs praeclārī iam in urbe _____.

_____

5. Cūr paene collāpsus es in caldāriō, Cornēlī?

Rogābant Cornēlium cūr in caldāriō paene _____.

_____

6. Cūr ē thermīs nunc ēgrederis, Cornēlī?

Rogābant Cornēlium cūr ē thermīs nunc _____.

_____

Applying What You Have Learned

Activity 43g Writing the Language

Translate the following English sentences into Latin. Include all long marks. Use the stories and vocabulary lists in your textbook, as well as the vocabulary lists in this book, to help you:

1. Titus, when he had arrived at the Neronean Baths, met his friends in the entrance passage.

_____

2. He wanted to know how his friends wanted to exercise themselves in the palaestra.

_____

3. Since the water in the frigidarium was very cold, Titus and his friends were not delaying there for much time.

_____

4. When Titus saw the old man wiping his hands on the head of a slave with long hair, he laughed for a long time.

_____

5. He wanted to know who the old man was and why he was doing a thing so ridiculous.

_____

Activity 43h Expanding Your English Vocabulary

For each italicized English word, give the Latin word to which the English word is related.
Then complete each sentence by filling in a word at the right. Finally, give the meaning of each
Latin word you write at the left:

Latin Word
Meaning of the Latin Word

If you ...

1. _____
_____

apply an *unguent* to a wound,
you smear a healing _____
on the wound.

_____

2. _____
_____

are causing *friction* to occur
between a towel and your skin,
you are _____ the towel
on your skin.

_____

3. _____
_____

are counting *calories* in your
diet, you are counting units
of energy or

_____

4. _____
_____

make a *terse* comment, you
make a comment that is
brief, with all unnecessary
words removed or _____ out.

_____

5. _____
_____

are using your *cognitive*
skills, you are engaged in a
_____ process.

_____

6. _____
_____

are in the *vestibule* of a
building, you are in the
_____ passage.

_____

7. _____
_____

are *cognizant* of a situation,
you are _____ of it.

_____

8. _____
_____

count using your *digits*, you
count on your

_____

9. _____
_____

are a *senior* citizen, you are
an _____ citizen.

_____

10. _____
_____

offer a *contrary* opinion, you
offer one that is _____
any already expressed.

_____

Name _____ Date _____ Period _____

Activity 43i Reading Latin

Look at the new vocabulary following this story. Then read the story, noting the **cum** *clauses, indirect questions, and subjunctives that are passive in form. Reread the story for comprehension. Then match the first part of each sentence that follows to the phrase or clause that correctly completes it:*

Bathing at Home

Cornēlia, quī pranderat et quiēverat, epistulam scrībēns in cubiculō sōla sedēbat. Cum puerī in urbem cum Eucleide ēgressī essent, domus Cornēliāna tranquilla erat. Etiam Cornēlius ad balneās vīcīnās profectus erat. Nihil audiēbātur nisi servī ancillaeque procul labōrantēs. Deinde ingressa est Aurēlia.

"Vīsne mēcum ad balneum nostrum īre, mea fīlia?"

"Ita vērō," respondit Cornēlia. "Lavārī tēcum mihi multum placet." Brevī tempore prōcēdēbant cum ancillīs māter fīliaque ad illam partem domūs ubi balneum fuit. Dum eō ambulant, Cornēlia mātrem rogāvit cūr in thermīs pūblicīs nōn lavārentur.

Aurēlia fīliae rem ita explicāvit. "Mulierēs quaedam in thermīs ante merīdiem lavārī solent, sed in thermīs lavārī mulierēs praeclārās nōn decet. Quamquam virī optimī ad thermās post merīdiem īre solent, mulierēs optimae tamen domī lavantur. Nōs igitur sīcut aliae tālēs Rōmānae in balneō nostrō domī lavārī solēmus."

Cum balneum ingressae essent et vestīmenta exuissent, in balneō calidō cōnsēdērunt. Cornēlia, cum cuperet cognōscere ubi esset Valerius et num ad urbem regressus esset, statim rogāvit, "Dīc mihi dē Valeriō, māter. Quid novī est?"

"Ille adulēscēns, quī iam convaluit, abhinc complūrēs diēs ad urbem pervēnit," respondit Aurēlia. "Hodiē in thermīs cum patre tuō convenīre voluit Valerius, ut crēdō."

"Is est adulēscēns optimus et fēlīcissimus, māter!" exclāmāvit Cornēlia. "Ubi fābulam ā servō eius nārrātam audīvī, perterrita fuī! Fortasse hūc ā patre

invītābitur, nam dē omnibus rēbus ab eō ipsō audīre volō." Diū Cornēlia et
Aurēlia multa dē Valeriō loquēbantur.

Tandem fēminae iam vestītae ā balneō profectae sunt. Dum silentiō
ambulābant, Cōrnēlia dē Valeriō cōgitābat et Aurēlia sē rogābat cūr tam multa ā
Cornēliā dē Valeriō dicta essent.

prandeō, prandēre, prandī, prānsus, *to eat lunch*
tranquillus, -a, -um, *peaceful*
balneum, -ī, n., *bathing room, bathing tub*
lavor, lavārī, lautus sum, *to bathe (oneself)*
decet, decēre, decuit, *it is right, proper, fitting*
sīcut, adv., *just as*
num, adv., *whether*
convalēscō, convalēscere, convaluī, *to grow stronger, get well*
vestītus, -a, -um, *clothed*

1. Cum Aurēlia in cubiculum Cornēliae ingressus esset... _____

2. Aurēlia Cornēliae explicāvit... _____

3. Cum fēminae optimae in thermīs nōn lavārentur... _____

4. Cum Cornēlia rogāvisset quid novī esset... _____

5. Fēminae, cum vestīmenta exuissent... _____

6. Cum fābula dē Valeriō ā servō nārrāta esset... _____

7. Cum Valerius iam in urbe morārētur... _____

a. Aurēlia explicāvit quōcum convenīret Cornēlius.

b. lavābantur.

c. fīliam rogāvit num lavārī vellet.

d. Cornēlia eum vidēre voluit.

e. Cornēlia et Aurēlia domī lavābantur.

f. Cornēlia perterrita fuit.

g. cūr in thermīs nōn lavārentur.

STOP THIEF!

In addition to vocabulary and the story, the activities in this chapter focus on:
1. present participles (review).
2. perfect passive participles.
3. the ablative absolute.
4. linking **quī**.

Web Code: jgd-0017

Vocabulary

Activity 44a Vocabulary

Study the vocabulary list on page 220 alone or with a partner.

The Story

Activity 44b Vocabulary in Context

Fill in the blanks with Latin words to match the English cues:

1. Proximō diē Asellus vestīmenta puerōrum in apodytēriō custōdiēbat, nam in thermīs sunt

   multī _____. (thieves)

2. Dum Asellus dormit, homō quīdam tunicam Sextī tacitē _____. (stole)

3. Sextus in apodytērium intrāns hominem cōnspexit et Asellō clāmāvit,

   "_____ eum!" (Seize)

4. Sextus fūrem _____. Asellus ē sellā _____. (followed)
   (leaped out)

5. Fūr in palaestram _____ et in pavīmentō _____.
   (fled for refuge) (slipped)

Present Participles (Review)

Activity 44c Present Participles as Modifiers

Fill in the blanks with present participles of the verbs in parentheses. Make the participle agree with the underlined noun or nouns in gender, case, and number. Then translate:

1. <u>Mārcus et Sextus</u> ē lūdō _____ inter sē colloquēbantur. (ēgredī)

_____

2. <u>Puerī</u> verba Eucleidis _____ cōgitābant, "Quam ērudītus est Eucleides!"
(audīre)

_____

3. Via ad thermās ferēns erat plēna <u>puerōrum</u> ē lūdō _____. (venīre)

_____

4. <u>Puerōs</u> in thermās _____ amīcī salūtāvērunt. (intrāre)

_____

5. <u>Puerīs</u> vestīmenta _____ Eucleidēs, "Nunc in palaestram exeāmus," inquit.
(exuere)

_____

_____

6. <u>Servō</u> vestīmenta _____ nōmen erat Asellus. (custōdīre)

_____

7. Magnus est numerus <u>fūrum</u> vestīmenta in hāc urbe _____. (surripere)

_____

8. Sextus <u>servō</u> vestīmenta _____ cōnfīdēbat. (custōdīre)

_____

9. Vestīmenta ā <u>servō</u> _____ nōn bene custōdīta sunt. (dormīre)

_____

10. <u>Sextus</u> ē tepidāriō _____ fūrem cōnspexit. (ēgredī)

_____

Building the Meaning

Verbs: Perfect Passive Participles II

Activity 44d Perfect Passive Participles as Modifiers

Combine the following sentences by reducing the first to a perfect passive participle and inserting it into the second. Include any other words from the first sentence needed to make sense. Then translate the new sentence into English. The first set is done for you.

1. Coquus vocātus est. Coquus ab omnibus laudātus est.

   Coquus vocātus ab omnibus laudātus est. _____

   The cook, summoned, was praised by everyone. _____

2. Coquus laudātus est. Coquus ad culīnam rediit.

   _____

   _____

3. Fūr captus est. Dominus īrā commōtus fūrī appropinquāvit.

   _____

   _____

4. Fūr captus est. Dominus ā fūre vestīmenta surrepta ēripuit.

   _____

   _____

5. Fūr captus est. Dominus in fronte fūris litterās FUR inūssit.

   _____

   _____

Ablative Absolutes

Activity 44e Ablative Absolutes

Combine the following sentences by transforming the first into an ablative absolute. Translate the new sentence. The first set is done for you.

1. Puerī verba Eucleidis audīvērunt. Puerī maximē gaudēbant.

   Verbīs Eucleidis audītīs, puerī maximē gaudēbant.

   When Eucleides' words had been heard, the boys were very happy.

2. Puerī vestīmenta exuērunt. Puerī in tepidārium intrāvērunt.

   _____

   _____

3. Puerī in tepidārium intrābant. Fūr vestīmenta surripuit.

   _____

   _____

4. Sextus aegrōtat. Puerī ē caldāriō ēgressī sunt.

   _____

   _____

5. Puerī in apodytērium ingrediēbantur. Fūr celeriter aufūgit cēlāvit.

   _____

   _____

6. Vestīmenta surrepta sunt. Sextus īrātus factus est.

   _____

   _____

7. Fūr aufugiēbat. Sextus magnā vōce clāmābat.

   _____

   _____

8. Sextus clāmābat. Fūr lāpsus in aquam cecidit.

_____

_____

9. Fūr captus est. Dominus Sextum laudāvit.

_____

_____

10. Litterae in fronte inūstae sunt. Fūr trīstis erat.

_____

_____

Building the Meaning

Linking *quī*

Activity 44f Sentences Beginning with Linking *quī*

Explain the thing, person, or action in the first sentence to which the linking **quī** *in the second sentence refers:*

1. Sextus Asellō, "Custōdī," inquit, "mea vestīmenta magnā cum cūrā." Quibus verbīs audītīs Asellus gemuit.

Explanation: _____

2. Fūr vestīmenta Sextī surripuit. Quod ubi vīdit Sextus, "Prehende illum fūrem!" exclāmāvit.

Explanation: _____

Applying What You Have Learned

Activity 44g Writing the Language

Translate the following English sentences into Latin. Include all long marks. Use the stories and vocabulary lists in your textbook, as well as the vocabulary lists in this book, to help you:

1. Asellus was telling the other slaves what had happened in the baths on that day.

_____

2. "I was watching Sextus's clothing with great care since there were many thieves.

_____

3. "Suddenly a very fierce thief leapt out of the entrance passage, and although I was on guard (use ablative absolute) he stole Sextus's clothing.

_____

4. "Having seen him (whom having been seen—use ablative absolute) I was terrified, but not Sextus: he followed the thief into the exercise ground.

_____

5. "The thief, having slipped on the pavement of the cold room, fell into the water, and Sextus was able to catch him."

_____

Activity 44h Expanding Your English Vocabulary

*Many English words can be traced back, often through French, to the Latin verb **prehendō, prehendere, prehendī, prehēnsus,** to seize, which is often compounded with prefixes. Give definitions of the following derivatives of this verb. Use an English dictionary as necessary. Note in each case how the meaning of the English word is related to that of the Latin verb and the prefix:*

1. to apprehend: _____

2. apprehensive: _____

3. apprentice: _____

_____

4. to apprise: _____

5. to comprehend: _____

6. to comprise: _____

7. emprise: _____

8. enterprise: _____

9. entrepreneur: _____

10. misapprehension: _____

11. prehensile: _____

12. prison: _____

_____

13. to reprehend: _____

14. reprehensible: _____

15. reprisal: _____

16. to surprise: _____

17. surprise _____

The following came into English through Italian:

18. impresario: _____

_____

Activity 44i Reading Latin

Look at the new vocabulary following this story. Then read the story, noting the use of ablative absolutes and linking **quī**. *Reread the story for comprehension. Then correct the statements that follow the story by rewriting them:*

Theater Invitation

Cornēliō epistulam in tablīnō scrībente, Aurēlia ingressus est et, "Crās erit

diēs fēstus. Lūdī scaenicī igitur in theātrō agentur. Vīsne mē ad theātrum dūcere?

Quis eō diē domī manēbit?"

Cornēlius, epistulā dēpositā, gemuit. "Lūdī scaenicī mihi nōn placent, ut

bene scīs, quod undique est nimis clāmōris, tumultūs, strepitūs. Lūdīs cōnfectīs,

ego semper aegrōtō."

Quibus tamen verbīs audītīs Aurēlia, "Cēterī senātōrēs uxōrēs suās ad theātrum dūcere solent. Ego quoque eō īre cupiō quoniam lūdī scaenicī mihi maximē placent. Ōlim enim fābulam Plautī facētam spectāvī et multum rīdēbam, nam nihil facētius spectāveram quam illam fābulam. Crās Aululāria Plautī in scaenā agētur."

Eōdem diē Cornēlius apud amīcum quendam cēnābat. Cēnā cōnfectā, inter sē colloquēbantur convīvae. Variī erant sermōnēs. Tandem Aemilius, ūnus ē convīvīs, "Iam tempus est," inquit, "cubitum īre, nam in animō habeō uxōrem fīliamque ad lūdōs scaenicōs crās māne dūcere. Vultisne tū et uxor nōbīscum īre, Cornēlī?"

Cornēlius, cum domum regressus esset, statim Aurēliam petīvit. Uxōre in cubiculō inventā, "Aurēlia," inquit, "sī ad lūdōs scaenicōs crās īre vīs, tē dūcam. Hoc, ut bene sciō, mea cārissima, tibi placēbit." Cui Aurēlia exclāmāvit, "Mihi valdē placēbit!" et maximō cum gaudiō marītum est amplexa et ōsculāta. "Stolam nūper ēmptam geram et cum amīcīs meīs diū colloquī poterō." Illā nocte cubitum iit Aurēlia lūdōs scaenicōs avidē exspectāns.

Postrīdiē māne igitur, uxōre novam stolam pallamque induente, Cornēlius togam praetextam induit. Omnibus rēbus parātīs, Cornēlius arcessīvit lectīcāriōs. Quī per viās urbis Cornēlium et Aurēliam ad theātrum Marcellī ferentēs summā celeritāte cucurrērunt. Cornēliī, cum in theātrum ingressī essent, in orchēstram ductī sunt ad illa subsellia prope scaenam sita ubi sedēbant senātōrēs cum uxōribus. Amīcīs comitantibus, Aurēlia Cornēliusque prīmam fābulam spectāre parāvērunt.

Cum prīmum histriōnēs in scaenam vēnērunt, magnā vōce clāmāvērunt spectātōrēs neque quisquam in tōtō theātrō tacēbat. Cornēlius prīmō gemuit, nam spectātōribus histriōnēs plaudentibus caput eī dolēbat. Mox tamen rīdēbat quod prīma fābula eī maximē placēbat.

In hāc fābulā nārrābātur dē sene avārō quī in domō suā habēbat multum aurī, quod in variīs locīs cēlāre cōnstituit. In fābulā erat etiam adulēscēns quī fīliam senis vehementissimē amābat. Servus eius adulēscentis cognōvit ubi esset aurum atque surripuit. Adulēscēns tamen aurum invēnit et senī reddidit. Laetissimus erat senex et fīliam adulēscentī uxōrem dedit.

Merīdiē propter calōrem sōlis vēlārium super capita spectātōrum sublātum est. Tandem, cum complūrēs fābulae essent āctae, aulaeum sublātum est ac cantor, "Vōs plaudite!" clāmāvit. Fābulae spectātae placēbant et Aurēliae et Cornēliō, quī paulum modo aegrōtābat.

fēstus, -a, -um, *festive, joyous*
  diēs fēstus, *holiday*
lūdī scaenicī, -ōrum, m. pl., *plays*
agentur, *(they) will be put on*
fābula, -ae, f., *story, play*
Plautus, -ī, m., *Plautus (a Roman playwright)*
facētus, -a, -um, *witty, humorous*
Aululāria, -ae, f., *Aulularia* (the name of a play by Plautus, with reference to a pot, **aula,** of gold that a miser hides in various places)
scaena, -ae, f., *stage*
sermō, sermōnis, m., *conversation, talk*
marītus, -ī, m., *husband*
amplector, amplectī, amplexus sum, *to hug, embrace*
ōsculor, -ārī, -ātus sum, *to kiss*
avidē, adv., *eagerly*
orchēstra, -ae, f., *orchestra* (the circular area where the chorus sang and danced in Greek theaters; the part of a Roman theater reserved for the seating of senators)
subsellium, -ī, n., *seat, bench*
comitor, -ārī, -ātus sum, *to accompany*
histriō, histriōnis, m., *actor*
quisquam, quaequam, quicquam or **quidquam,** *anyone, anything*
plaudō, plaudere, plausī, plausus, *to clap, applaud*

    caput eī dolēbat, *the head began to hurt for him, his head began to ache*
    avārus, -a, -um, *miserly*
    sōl, sōlis, m., *sun*
    vēlārium, -ī, n., *awning (over an open-air theater)*
    tollō, tollere, sustulī, sublātus, irreg., *to lift, raise*
    aulaeum, -ī, n., *curtain*
    cantor, cantōris, m., *player, musician*

1. Aurēlia, dum epistulam scrībit, tablīnum īntrāvit.

    _____

2. Ante lūdōs scaenicōs Cornēlius semper aegrōtābat.

    _____

3. Fābulā Plautī facētā explicātā, Aurēlia Cornēliusque multum rīdēbant.

    _____

4. Convīvae, dum cēnābant, variīs sermōnibus inter sē colloquēbantur.

    _____

5. Lectīcāriīs stantibus, Cornēlius Aurēliaque per viās urbis celeriter lātī sunt.

    _____

6. Histriōnibus ingressīs, spectātōrēs in tōtō theātrō tacuērunt.

    _____

7. Adulēscēns aurum senis avārī surripuit.

    _____

8. Senex fīliam servō uxōrem dedit.

    _____

9. Complūribus fābulīs āctīs, aulaeō sublātō, cantor plausit.

    _____

PYRAMUS AND THISBE

In addition to vocabulary and the story, the activities in this chapter focus on:
1. future active participles.
2. participles (consolidation).
3. Ovid's story of Pyramus and Thisbe.

Web Code: jgd-0018

Vocabulary

Activity 45a Vocabulary

Study the vocabulary list on pages 221–222 alone or with a partner.

The Story

Activity 45b Vocabulary in Context

Fill in the blanks with Latin words to match the English cues:

1. Pȳramus Thisbēque, parentibus _____, alter alterī amōrem

_____ et multa _____ per rīmam in pariete domuī

_____ commūnī sitam dabant. (not knowing) (were expressing)
(kisses) (each)

2. Tum _____ et adulēscēns in silvam sē illā nocte conventūrōs esse pollicitī

_____. (maiden) (said goodbye)

3. Nam diē _____ Pȳramus et Thisbē _____

_____. (previous) (had adopted a plan)

4. Itaque, ubi lūna oriēbātur, Thisbē silentiō noctis _____ suum vēlāmine

cēlāvit et in silvam _____. (face) (went forward)

5. Ēheu! Leō vēnit, nōn Pȳramus! Itaque Thisbē timōrem magnum _____
in spēluncam cōnfūgit. (feeling)

6. Pȳramus sērō advēnit, et, vēstīgiīs leōnis et Thisbēs vīsīs, exclāmāvit moritūrus,

"_____ Thisbēn! _____ virginem cārissimam!"
(I have killed) (I have destroyed)

Forms

Future Participles

Activity 45c Forming Future Active Participles

Using the participial form in the first column, form the future active participle. Then translate the participle you have just written:

Non-deponent Verbs

Perfect Passive Participle   **Future Active Participle**   **Translation**

1. perditus, -a, -um   _____   _____

2. sēnsus, -a, -um   _____   _____

Deponent Verbs

Perfect Participle   **Future Active Participle**   **Translation**

3. pollicitus, -a, -um   _____   _____

4. prōgressus, -a, -um   _____   _____

Building the Meaning

Participles (Consolidation)

Activity 45d Participles in Context

For each sentence, select the participle that correctly translates the italicized phrase:

1. *Having gone forth* into the woods, Thisbe wondered why Pyramus had not yet arrived.

_____

   prōgrediēns   prōgressa   prōgressūra

2. *Going forth* into the woods, Thisbe walked silently. _____

   prōgrediēns   prōgressa   prōgressūra

3. *About to go forth* into the woods, Thisbe prayed to the gods. _____

prōgrediēns   prōgressa   prōgressūra

4. The lion, *having followed* Thisbe, seized her veil. _____

sequēns   secūtus   secūtūrus

5. Pyramus saw the veil *spattered* with blood. _____

aspergēns   aspersum   aspersūrum

Applying What You Have Learned

Activity 45e Reading the Language

The following are extracts from the story of Pyramus and Thisbe as told by the Roman poet Ovid (Metamorphoses IV.55–166). The meter is dactylic hexameter. Write translations of the extracts on a separate sheet or sheets of paper. You may use the vocabulary at the back of your textbook in addition to the vocabulary and aids that are given with each Latin passage:

1. *The characters and setting:*

1 Pȳramus et Thisbē, iuvenum pulcherrimus alter,

2 altera, quās Oriēns habuit, praelāta puellīs,

3 contiguās tenuēre domōs, ubi dīcitur altam

4 coctilibus mūrīs cīnxisse Semīramis urbem.

       1 **iuvenis, iuvenis,** m., *young man*

       2 **quās**: the antecedent is **puellīs** at the end of the line.

          Oriēns, Orientis, m., *the eastern part of the world, the orient*

          praelātus, -a, -um + dat., *preferred to, excelling*

       3 **contiguus, -a, -um,** *neighboring, adjoining*

          tenuēre = tenuērunt

       4 **coctilis, -is, -e,** *made of sun-baked bricks*

          cingō, cingere, cīnxī, cīnctus, *to surround*

          Semīramis, Semīramidis, f., *Semiramis (a legendary ninth century B.C. queen of Assyria, who was said to have built the city of Babylon)*

2. *Thisbe, having gone out to the woods to meet Pyramus, sees a lioness:*

5 Quam procul ad lūnae radiōs Babylōnia Thisbē

6 vīdit et obscūrum timidō pede fūgit in antrum,

7 dumque fugit, tergō vēlāmina lāpsa relīquit.

5 **Quam**: i.e., *the lioness* (**leaena, -ae**, f.)

 ad, prep. + acc., here, *by the light of*

 radius, -ī, m., *ray, beam*

6 **obscūrus, -a, -um,** *dark*

 antrum, -ī, n., *cave*

7 **tergō = ā tergō**

 vēlāmina: plural for singular (common in Latin poetry)

3. *A short time later, Pyramus comes into the woods and finds the veil that the lioness had seen and torn with its bloody mouth:*

8 Pӯramus ut vērō vestem quoque sanguine tīnctam

9 repperit, "Ūna duōs," inquit, "nox perdet amantēs,

10 ē quibus illa fuit longā dignissima vītā;

11 nostra nocēns anima est. Ego tē, miseranda, perēmī,

12 in loca plēna metūs quī iussī nocte venīrēs

13 nec prior hūc vēnī."

 8 **ut,** *when*

 tīnctus, -a, -um, *wet, stained*

 9 **reperiō, reperīre, repperī, repertus,** *to find*

 10 **dignus, -a, -um** + abl., *worthy of*

 vīta, -ae, f., *life*

 11 **nostra = mea**

 nocēns, nocentis, *guilty*

 miserandus, -a, -um, *pitiable*

 perimō, perimere, perēmī, perēmptus, *to destroy*

 12 **venīrēs**: *(that) you should come*

4. *After Pyramus stabs himself, Thisbe comes out of hiding and finds the body of her lover:*

14 "Pӯrame," clāmāvit, "quis tē mihi cāsus adēmit?

15 Pӯrame, respondē! Tua tē cārissima Thisbē

16 nōminat; exaudī vultūsque attolle iacentēs!"

17 Ad nōmen Thisbēs oculōs ā morte gravātōs

18 Pӯramus ērēxit vīsāque recondidit illā.

 14 **quis**: interrogative adjective, modifying **cāsus**

 cāsus, -ūs, m., *accident, misfortune*

 16 **exaudiō, exaudīre, exaudīvī, exaudītus,** *to listen*

attollō, attollere, *to lift up*

17 **gravātus, -a, -um,** *weighed down*

18 **ērigō, ērigere, ērēxī, ērēctus,** *to lift up,* raise

recondō, recondere, recondidī, reconditus, *to put back again, to stow away;*
   to close (the eyes) again

5. *Upon realizing what had happened, Thisbe decided to die with her lover:*

19 "Persequar extīnctum lētīque miserrima dīcar

20 causa comesque tuī: quīque ā mē morte revellī

21 (heu!) sōlā poterās, poteris nec morte revellī."

19 **persequor, persequī, persecūtus sum,** *to follow*

extīnctus, -a, -um, *dead* (supply **tē** with **extīnctum**)

lētum, -ī, n., *death*

20 **comes, comitis,** m./f., *companion*

quīque, *and (you) who*

revellō, revellere, revellī, revulsus, *to tear away, remove*

21 **heu!** interj., *alas!*

6. *Before killing herself, Thisbe prayed on behalf of Pyramus and herself that they would be buried in the same tomb and that the fruit of the mulberry tree under which they died would henceforth be funereal black rather than its former white:*

22 Vōta tamen tetigēre deōs, tetigēre parentēs;

23 nam color in pōmō est, ubi permātūruit, āter,

24 quodque rogīs superest, ūnā requiēscit in urnā.

22 **vōtum, -ī,** n., *prayer*

tangō, tangere, tetigī, tāctus, *to touch* (**tetigēre = tetigērunt**)

23 **pōmum, -ī,** n., *fruit*

permātūrēscō, permātūrēscere, permātūruī, *to ripen fully*

āter, ātra, ātrum, *black*

24 **quodque,** *and (that) which*

rogus, -ī, m., *funeral pyre* (plural for singular here)

supersum, superesse, superfuī, *to be left over, remain*

requiēscō, requiēscere, requiēvī, requiētūrus, *to rest*

urna, -ae, f., *funerary urn*

A RAINY DAY

> *In addition to vocabulary and the story, the activities in this chapter focus on:*
> 1. the accusative and infinitive construction.
> 2. the irregular verb **fīō, fierī, factus sum**.

Go Online
PHSchool.com
Web Code: jgd-0019

Vocabulary

Activity 46a Vocabulary

Study the vocabulary list on page 223 alone or with a partner.

The Story

Activity 46b Vocabulary in Context

Fill in the blanks with Latin words to match the English cues:

1. "_____ ad Campum Mārtium, Mārce, dēscendere vīs, ubi pluit?" rogat Sextus. (Surely… not?)

2. _____ _____ latrunculīs duās _____ hōrās lūdēbant. (Both) (boys) (almost)

3. "Quid _____ _____ fīliae Dāvī?" Aurēliam rogat Cornēlia, nam diēs nātālis eius adest. (will I give as a gift)

4. "_____ pūpam fīliam Dāvī dēlectātūram esse, Cornēlia?" respondit Aurēlia. (Do you think?)

5. Ubi Sextus pūpam _____, Cornēlia exclāmāvit, "_____ meam pūpam _____!" (snatched away) (Don't . . . hurt)

6. _____ Cornēlius vēnit et Sextum pūpam Cornēliae reddere iussit. (Finally)

7. Sī Cornēlius īrātus erit, quid Sextō _____? (will happen)

Building the Meaning

Accusative and Infinitive (Indirect Statement) I

Activity 46c The Accusative and Infinitive Construction

Combine the two sentences in each set. The first set is done for you:

1. Dāvus est īrācundus. Quid dīcis?

   Dīcō Dāvum esse īrācundum. _____

2. Sextus est puer temerārius. Quid dīcis?

   Dīcō _____

3. Pater Mārcī est crūdēlis. Quid putat Sextus?

   Sextus putat _____

4. Cornēlius est senātor Rōmānus. Quid dīcitis?

   Dīcimus _____

5. Adstantēs fūrem ex aquā extrahunt. Quid vidēs?

   Videō _____

6. Sextus pūpam abripit. Quid Eucleidēs videt?

   Eucleidēs videt _____

7. Cornēlia pūpā lūdit. Quid Sextus crēdit?

   Sextus crēdit _____

8. Puerī molestissimī fīunt. Quid Eucleidēs sentit?

   Eucleidēs sentit _____

9. Puerī digitīs micant et magnā vōce clāmant. Quid Aurēlia et Cornēlia audiunt?

   Aurēlia et Cornēlia audiunt _____

10. Sextus fūrem subsequitur. Quid Asellus videt?

    Asellus videt _____

Forms

The Irregular Verb *fīō, fierī, factus sum*

Activity 46d Practice with Forms of *fīō*

Fill in the blanks with forms of **fīō** *to match the English cues:*

1. Quid Sextō _____? (will happen)

2. Clāmōribus puerōrum in ātriō audītīs, Cornēlius īrātus _____. (becomes)

3. Quod semper pluēbat, puerī trīstēs _____. (had become)

4. Pūpā abreptā, Cornēlia sollicita _____. (became)

5. Cornēlia mātrī, "Puerī," inquit, "_____ molestī." (are becoming)

6. Aurēlia, "Sī puerī nōn tacēbunt," inquit, "īrāta _____." (I will become)

Applying What You Have Learned

Activity 46e Writing the Language

Translate the following English sentences into Latin. Include all long marks. Use the stories and vocabulary lists in your textbook, as well as the vocabulary lists in this book, to help you:

1. What is happening to Canus (**Cānus, -ī,** m.)?

   _____

2. The emperor ordered him to be killed, but they say that he is unconcerned.

   _____

3. Everyone knows that even with his guards he is quietly playing the game of bandits and counting his pawns (**calculus, -ī,** m).

   _____

   _____

4. The guards believe that Canus is winning, even (when) advancing to his death.

   _____

5. Seneca thinks that Canus is a very brave man.

   _____

Activity 46f Expanding Your English Vocabulary

Using the word bank below, write the word that could replace the italicized word or words in each sentence. Use the Latin words in parentheses to help determine the meaning of the English words. Then write the English translation of each Latin word in the word bank:

1. Cornelia has *both positive and negative* feelings about the city of Rome. _____

2. Palaemon is *thought* to be a fine teacher. _____

3. Pseudolus did not *reckon* what his losses might be if his scheme were to be discovered by Aurelia. _____

4. Pirates are generally unconcerned with their *public image*. _____

5. Certain diseases can cause *sores* on the skin. _____

6. Some wealthy Romans *gave gifts of* temples to localities sacred to the gods. _____

7. Although Valerius was the *supposed* heir to a large fortune, he did not offer any reward to the pirates. _____

8. In theory at least, the Roman constitution provided *equality* of power between the two consuls. _____

lesions (**laedere**) _____	reputation (**putāre**) _____
parity (**pār**) _____	putative (**putāre**) _____
donated (**dōnum**) _____	ambivalent (**ambō**) _____
reputed (**putāre**) _____	compute (**putāre**) _____

Activity 46g Reading Latin

*Look at the new vocabulary following this story. Then read the story, noting the indirect statements. Reread the story for comprehension. Then mark whether each statement about the story is V = **Vērum** (True) or F = **Falsum** (False):*

A Gentle Reminder to Cornelius

Sextō trīstissimō ad cubiculum regressō, Cornēlius manibus caput tenēns in tablīnō sedēbat. Tum in tablīnum ingressus est Titus.

Titus: Cūr ita sedēs, mī Cornēlī? Cūr Sextus tam trīstis exiit? Quid accidit?

Cornēlius: Ēheu! Mihi necesse erat iterum Sextum pūnīre, nam pūpam ā Cornēliā factam ab eā abripuit et ex ātriō effūgit.

Titus:	Certē per iocum hoc fēcit Sextus. Num pūpam Cornēliae laesit?
Cornēlius:	Cum eum statim ad ātrium redīre iussissem, pūpam incolumem rettulit. Pūpā Cornēliae redditā, mēcum hūc Sextum redūxī et pūnīvī. Sentiō mē Sextum semper aut reprehendere aut pūnīre!
Titus:	Fortasse Sextum nimis pūnīre solēs. Puer scelestus Sextus nōn est.
Cornēlius:	Sextus autem pūpillus meus est, et ego sum tūtor eius. Pūpillī tūtōribus semper parēre dēbent. Mihi necesse est Sextum bene īnstituere, id quod difficillimum est.
Titus:	Tenēsne in memoriā Sextum adhūc puerum esse? Tenēsne in memoriā Sextum virum nōndum esse? Dīc mihi, Cornēlī, tenēsne in memoriā pueritiam tuam? Saepe tū sorōrem nostram vexābās, saepe in lūdō nōn bene tē gerēbās, saepe ā patre nostrō reprehendēbāris et pūniēbāris. Esne immemor hārum rērum? Sextus errāvit. Errāre hūmānum est.
Cornēlius:	Dīcisne Sextum pūnīrī nōn dēbēre?
Titus:	Dīcō omnēs puerōs errāre. Mementō Sextum puerum esse et tē ōlim fuisse puerum. Mementō tē esse hominem et hominis tūtōrem.

pūpillus, -ī, m., *ward*
tūtor, tūtōris, m., *guardian*
īnstituō, īnstituere, īnstituī, īnstitūtus, *to build up, educate, train*
id quod, *that/a thing which*
pueritia, -ae, f., *boyhood, childhood*
bene sē gerere, *to behave oneself well*
meminī, meminisse, *to remember*
  mementō, imperative
fuisse, *were*
homō, hominis, m., *man, human being*

1. Titus videt Sextum trīstem sedēre.   V   F

2. Titus crēdit Cornēlium Sextum semper pūnīre aut reprehendere.   V   F

3. Cornēlius crēdit tūtōrēs pūpillīs parēre dēbēre.   V   F

4. Difficile est Cornēliō Sextum bene īnstituere.   V   F

5. Titus dīcit Sextum adhūc puerum neque virum esse.   V   F

6. Cornēlius est homō et tūtor hominis.   V   F

LOOKING FORWARD TO THE GAMES

Go Online
PHSchool.com
Web Code: jgd-0020

In addition to vocabulary and the story, the activities in this chapter focus on:
1. the accusative and infinitive construction with future infinitives and with perfect active infinitives.
2. the irregular verb **mālō, mālle, māluī.**

Vocabulary

Activity 47a Vocabulary

Study the vocabulary list on page 224 alone or with a partner.

The Story

Activity 47b Vocabulary in Context

Fill in the blanks with Latin words to match the English cues:

1. Cornēlius Titō sē _____ esse dīcit. (very busy)

2. Titus frātrem ad _____ itūrum esse _____. (the games) (he hopes)

3. Cornēlius scit Aurēliam domī manēre _____. (prefers)

4. _____ servōs amphitheātrum summā celeritāte cōnfēcisse. (It is agreed)

5. Amphitheātrum tōtum populum _____ nōn potest. (to contain)

6. Cornēlius, "Plūrimī gladiātōrēs," inquit, "_____ mox salūtābunt." (emperor)

7. "Sextus domī manēbit," inquit Cornēlius, "nam, ut Seneca docet, _____

   populus, _____ perīculī." (the greater) (the more)

Building the Meaning

Accusative and Infinitive (Indirect Statement) II

Activity 47c Indirect Statement

Underline the indirect statement in each complete sentence. Then complete the other sentences with present, perfect, or future infinitives as appropriate. The first set is done for you:

1. Titus dīcit <u>sē ad mūnera heri īvisse</u>.

   Titus dīcit sē ad mūnera hodiē *īre*____.

   Titus dīcit sē ad mūnera crās *itūrum esse*____.

2. Titus dīcit multōs cīvēs mūnera heri vīdisse.

   Titus dīcit multōs cīvēs mūnera hodiē _____.

   Titus dīcit multōs cīvēs mūnera crās _____.

3. Titus cognōscit frātrem negōtiōsum heri _____.

   Titus cognōscit frātrem negōtiōsum hodiē _____.

   Titus cognōscit frātrem negōtiōsum crās futūrum esse.

4. Crēdimus Titum ad mūnera heri _____.

   Crēdimus Titum ad mūnera hodiē advenīre.

   Crēdimus Titum ad mūnera crās _____.

5. Gāius Cornēlius prō certō habet servōs amphitheātrum heri cōnfēcisse.

   Gāius Cornēlius prō certō habet servōs amphitheātrum hodiē _____.

   Gāius Cornēlius prō certō habet servōs amphitheātrum crās _____.

6. Cōnstat Aurēliam domī heri _____.

   Cōnstat Aurēliam domī hodiē manēre.

   Cōnstat Aurēliam domī crās _____.

7. Mārcus dīcit Cornēlium ad mūnera sē heri _____.

Mārcus dīcit Cornēlium ad mūnera sē hodiē _____.

Mārcus dīcit Cornēlium ad mūnera sē crās ductūrum esse.

8. Scīmus Sextum domī heri manēre _____.

Scīmus Sextum domī hodiē manēre nōlle.

9. Scīmus Sextum heri ad mūnera īre _____.

Scīmus Sextum hodiē ad mūnera īre velle.

Forms

The Irregular Verb *mālō, mālle, māluī*

Activity 47d Practice with Forms of *mālō*

Supply appropriate forms of **mālō**:

1. CORNĒLIUS: Vīsne ad mūnera crās īre, Aurēlia?

2. AURĒLIA: Ego domī manēre _____.

3. CORNĒLIUS: _____, Mārce, ad mūnera īre an domī manēre?

4. AURĒLIA: Mārcus certē ad mūnera īre _____ quam domī manēre.

5. MĀRCUS: Ego et Titus ad mūnera īre _____ quam domī manēre.

6. AURĒLIA: _____, Cornēlia et Sexte, ad mūnera īre an domī manēre?

7. CORNĒLIUS: Cornēlia et Sextus ad mūnera īre _____ sed domī manēre dēbent.

an, conj., *or*

Applying What You Have Learned

Activity 47e Writing the Language

Translate the following English sentences into Latin. Include all long marks. Use the stories and vocabulary lists in your textbook, as well as the vocabulary lists in this book, to help you:

1. Titus is sure that Cornelius will not work tomorrow.

   _____

2. Titus hopes that Cornelius will go to the games tomorrow.

   _____

3. He does not realize that his brother said this as a joke.

   _____

4. Everyone knows that slaves finished the amphitheater.

   _____

5. I hope that we will see you in the amphitheater.

   _____

Activity 47f Expanding Your Latin and English Vocabularies

1. *Using a Latin dictionary, find meanings for the following:*

   ōtium   _____

   ōtiōsus   _____

   ōtiōsē   _____

   ōtior   _____

2. *Using an English dictionary, find the meaning of the following:*

   otiose   _____

3. *Using a Latin dictionary, find meanings for the following:*

   negōtium   _____

   negōtiōsus _____

negōtiātiō _____

negōtiātor _____

negōtior _____

4. *Explain the relationship between the words* **ōtium** *and* **negōtium:**

_____

_____

5. *Give meanings for the following English words (use a dictionary as necessary):*

negotiate _____

negotiation _____

negotiator _____

negotiable _____

negotiant _____

Activity 47g Reading Latin

Look at the new vocabulary following this story. Then read the story, noting the different infinitive tenses used in indirect statements. Reread the story for comprehension. Then answer the questions that follow with complete Latin sentences.

Both Sides of the Games

Cum Titus ē tablīnō discessisset, servus ā Cornēliō arcessītus, nōmine Tīrō, ingressus est et dominum negōtiōsum invēnit.

Cornēlius: Hās epistulās statim cōnficere mihi necesse est, nam prō certō habeō mē paulum modo labōris crās cōnfectūrum esse. Ad mūnera Mārcum mēcum dūcam, itaque crās multum temporis ad negōtium nōn habēbō.

Tīrō: Diū omnēs haec mūnera avidē exspectant, et cōnstat amphitheātrum Flāvium futūrum esse glōriam populī Rōmānī. Magna pars populī Rōmānī in illō amphitheātrō continērī poterit.

Cornēlius: Nōs omnēs cīvēs haec mūnera maximē magnifica memorābiliaque futūra esse spērāmus.

Tīrō: Sentiō certāmina gladiātōrum tibi placēre. Quī gladiātōrēs tibi placent?

Cornēlius:	Duo lībertī, nōmine Ōceanus Albānusque, quī complūrēs annōs optimē pugnāvērunt, mihi multum placent. Etiam audiō gladiātōrem quendam, nōmine Sevērum, saepissimē vīcisse, quamquam ego ipse eum in arēnā pugnantem numquam vīdī. Crēscēns dīcitur multōs adversāriōs superāvisse et in novō amphitheātrō crās pugnātūrus esse. Semper mihi placet spectāre virōs quī bene pugnant atque perīculō mortīque fortiter obviam eunt. Mortem tamen miserrimōrum captīvōrum in arēnā cum bēstiīs pugnantium spectāre mihi nōn placet.
Tīrō:	Audiō captīvōs quōsdam mortem tam taetram veritōs ante certāmen sē necāvisse.
Cornēlius:	Nōn semper mihi placent mūnera, nam clāmōre strepitūque semper aeger fīō. Placet igitur mihi domī cum Aurēliā nōnnumquam manēre neque mūnera spectāre.

negōtium, -ī, n., *business*
    ad negōtium, *for business*
avidē, adv., *eagerly*
certāmen, certāminis, n., *contest*
pugnō, -āre, -āvī, -ātūrus, *to fight*
adversārius, -ī, m., *opponent, adversary*
obviam īre + dat., *to face, go out to meet*
bēstia, -ae, f., *wild beast*
taeter, taetra, taetrum, *foul, horrible*
nōnnumquam, adv., *sometimes*

1. Quid crās Cornēlius faciet?

_____

2. Quid Tīrō dīcit amphitheātrum novum contentūrum esse?

_____

3. Quid Cornēlius dīcit Ōceanum Albānumque fēcisse?

_____

4. Quis in amphitheātrō Flāviō crās pugnābit?

_____

5. Quōs virōs spectāre Cornēliō nōn placet?

_____

_____

6. Cūr captīvī sē necāvērunt?

_____

7. Quam ob rem aeger fit Cornēlius?

_____

8. Quid Cornēlius agere māvult?

_____

A DAY AT THE COLOSSEUM

Go Online
PHSchool.com
Web Code: jgd-0021

In addition to vocabulary and the story, the activities in this chapter focus on:
1. infinitives (consolidation).
2. the accusative and infinitive construction introduced by verbs in a past tense.
3. the accusative and infinitive construction with passive infinitives and infinitives of deponent verbs.
4. subordinate constructions (review).

Vocabulary

Activity 48a Vocabulary

Study the vocabulary list on pages 225–226 alone or with a partner.

The Story

Activity 48b Vocabulary in Context

Fill in the blanks with Latin words to match the English cues:

1. Cornēlius tesserās appāritōribus _____. (showed)

2. Mārcus _____ hominēs nōn prius vīderat. (so many)

3. Gladiātōrēs sē _____, _____, oculōs ad pulvīnar

   _____. (turned) (stopped) (raised)

4. Cum gladiātōrēs _____ pulvīnar cōnstitissent, magnopere clāmābātur. (opposite)

5. In _____ _____ et fortiter pugnābātur. (arena) (fiercely)

6. Mārcus _____ quot gladiātōrēs pugnārent. (was guessing)

7. Mārcus _____ merīdiānōrum aliās vidēbit. (the frenzy)

Name _____ Date _____ Period _____

Forms

Verbs: Infinitives (Consolidation)

Activity 48c Forming Infinitives

Write the requested forms of the infinitive for each verb below:

Present Active	Present Passive	Perfect Active	Perfect Passive	Future Active
1. spērāre	_____	_____	_____	_____
2. dēlēre	_____	_____	_____	_____
3. convertere	_____	_____	_____	_____
4. conicere	_____	_____	_____	_____
5. sepelīre	_____	_____	_____	_____

Deponent Verbs

Present	Perfect	Future
1. cōnārī	_____	_____
2. pollicērī	_____	_____
3. lābī	_____	_____
4. prōgredī	_____	_____
5. adorīrī	_____	_____

Building the Meaning

Accusative and Infinitive (Indirect Statement) III and IV

Activity 48d Passive Infinitives and Infinitives of Deponent Verbs in Indirect Statements after Introductory Verbs in Present and Past Tenses

Translate the following into English, paying particular attention to the tenses of the introductory verbs and the infinitives:

1. Mārcus dīcit patrem epistulam cōnfēcisse.

2. Mārcus dīxit patrem epistulam cōnfēcisse.

_____

3. Mārcus dīcit patrem epistulam crās cōnfectūrum esse.

_____

4. Mārcus dīxit epistulam ā patre cōnfectam esse.

_____

5. Mārcus dīcit epistulam ā patre cōnficī.

_____

6. Mārcus dīxit epistulam ā patre cōnficī.

_____

7. Videō Titum ad amphitheātrum festīnāre.

_____

8. Audīvī Titum ad amphitheātrum festīnāvisse.

_____

9. Audīvī Titum ad amphitheātrum festīnātūrum esse.

_____

10. Audīvī Sextum Mārcum ad mūnera secūtum esse.

_____

11. Putāvī Sextum Mārcum ad mūnera secūtūrum esse.

_____

12. Vīdī Cornēliam gladiātōrēs magnopere verērī.

_____

13. Scīvī Sextum et Mārcum gladiātōrēs numquam veritūrōs esse.

_____

14. Audīvī prīncipem saepe ā gladiātōribus salūtātum esse.

_____

15. Mārcus spērat patrem sē ad amphitheātrum iterum ductūrum esse.

_____

Activity 48e Review: *Cum* Circumstantial Clauses, Ablative Absolutes, and Accusative and Infinitive Constructions

Underline the subordinate construction in each of the following Latin sentences. Then translate sentence "a" and use its construction as a model for translating sentence "b."

1. a. Cum Titus ad amphitheātrum pervēnisset, multōs amīcōs vīdit.

_____

b. When we had entered the amphitheater, a thief stole our money.

_____

2. a. Nesciēbāmus quis pecūniam nostram surripuisset.

_____

b. We did not know where **(quō)** the thief had fled.

_____

3. a. Imperātōre intrante omnēs surrēxērunt.

_____

b. When the gladiators were entering, all the spectators began to shout.

_____

4. a. Nōn crēdō Cornēliam mūnera amāre.

_____

b. I know that she will not go to the games.

_____

5. a. Crēdēbam Titum Mārcum ad mūnera ōlim dūxisse.

_____

b. I thought that Titus would take Marcus to the games tomorrow.

_____

Applying What You Have Learned

Activity 48f Writing the Language

Translate the following English sentences into Latin. Include all long marks. Use the stories and vocabulary lists in your textbook, as well as the vocabulary lists in this book, to help you:

1. Titus said that Hermes (**Hermēn**) was a cause of fright to all gladiators.

_____

2. Since he had killed so many gladiators, Hermes was very arrogant. (Use a **cum** causal clause.)

_____

3. When Hermes was marching in wearing his plumed metal helmet, the crowd called him the delight of the age. (Use a **cum** circumstantial clause.)

_____

4. Titus knew Sextus preferred to go to the games than to go to school.

_____

5. Titus promised that he would soon take Sextus to the amphitheater.

_____

Activity 48g Expanding Your English Vocabulary

Using the following word bank, write the word that could replace the italicized word or words in each sentence. Use the Latin words in parentheses to help determine the meaning of the English words. Then write the English translation of each Latin word in the word bank:

1. Cornelius's house was elegant, but it avoided the *showy* display of wealth.

_____

2. Marcus was trying to make a *guess* as to how many spectators the amphitheater held.

_____

3. Pseudolus's *apparent* purpose was to buy a pig, but his real purpose was to make a profit for himself.

_____

4. What had originally been the site of a lake on the grounds of Nero's Domus Aurea was now *turned* into the site of the amphitheater.

_____

5. The slaves sometimes feel the sting of Cornelius's *anger*.

_____

6. When he was caught, the thief was not *combative*; he gave up without a fight.

_____

7. In a triumph, a victorious general was *lifted up in praise* by the people.

_____

8. Most Romans did not consider gladiatorial fights morally *offensive*.

_____

9. Palaemon had a *fiercely bitter* dispute with Sextus.

_____

10. Some Roman art was religious, but a great deal of it was *worldly*.

_____

acrimonious (**ācriter**) _____	repugnant (**pugnāre**) _____
ostentatious (**ostendere**) _____	conjecture (**conicere**) _____
extolled (**tollere**) _____	secular (**saeculum**) _____
ostensible (**ostendere**) _____	converted (**convertere**) _____
fury (**furor**) _____	pugnacious (**pugnāre**) _____

Activity 48h Reading Latin

Look at the new vocabulary following this story. Then read the story, noting the accusatives and infinitives in indirect statements. Reread the story for comprehension. Then correct the following statements about the story by rewriting the sentences:

Good Games and Bad

Mārcus, cum domum regressus esset, cum Cornēliā Eucleideque dē mūneribus eō diē vīsīs loquēbātur.

Cornēlia: Tibi placuērunt mūnera et amphitheātrum, Mārce?

Mārcus: Quam ingēns est amphitheātrum! Tot dēliciae! Tot mīlia spectātōrum! Nōn sōlum multōs et variōs hominēs, sed etiam Caesarem ipsum in pulvīnārī sedentem vīdī! Pater dīxit sē prīncipem ibi saepe vīdisse, nam Caesarī quoque mūnera placent.

Eucleidēs:	Quid dē gladiātōribus? Bene in arēnā pugnābātur?
Mārcus:	Ferōciter pugnābātur! Paria gladiātōrum, cum in arēnam incessissent, magnō cum furōre pugnāvērunt! Murmillōnēs rētiāriīque mihi placuērunt, quamquam Thraecibus maximē fāvit Titus patruus. Titus mihi dīxit illōs quōs vīdissēmus esse gladiātōrēs bonōs, sed optimōs post merīdiem pugnātūrōs esse. Pugnīs vīsīs, putō omnēs gladiātōrēs bonōs fuisse.
Cornēlia:	Pater saepe dīcit patruum nostrum plūra dē gladiātōribus aurīgīsque quam dē rēbus urbānīs scīre.
Mārcus:	(cum rīsū) Ille certē ad mūnera aut lūdōs quam ad Cūriam īre māvult atque nōmina et victōriās omnium gladiātōrum scit.
Eucleidēs:	Nōn omnēs gladiātōrēs sunt bonī pugnātōrēs neque omnia mūnera optima sunt. Scrīptor quīdam, Petrōnius nōmine, dē mūneribus scrīpsit in quibus pugnābant gladiātōrēs dēcrepitī īnfirmīque quī, sī eōs sufflāvissēs, cecidissent. Scrīpsit ūnum ex gladiātōribus fuisse simillimum gallō, alium lōripidem, tertium paene mortuum. Thraex sōlus paulō impigrior erat sed ad dictāta modo pugnāvit. Tandem, spectātōribus incitantibus, tōta turba gladiātōrum verberāta est!
Mārcus:	Titus patruus affirmāvit tālia mūnera numquam in urbe sed saepe in oppidīs vidērī. Spērō mē merīdiānōs ferōcissimōs in amphitheātrō pugnantēs brevī tempore spectātūrum esse.
Cornēlia:	Domī cum mātre morārī mālam!

nōn sōlum...sed etiam, *not only...but also*

murmillō, murmillōnis, m., *fish man (a type of gladiator)*

rētiārius, -ī, m., *net man (a type of gladiator)*

Thraex, Thraecis, m., *Thracian (a type of gladiator)*

pugna, -ae, f., *fight*

pugnātor, pugnātōris, m., *fighter, combatant*

scrīptor, scrīptōris, m., *writer*

dēcrepitus, -a, -um, *decrepit, worn out, broken down*

sufflō, -āre, -āvī, -ātus, *to blow on*

    sī eōs sufflāvissēs, cecidissent, *if you had blown on them, they would have fallen*

gallus, -ī, m., *rooster*

lōripēs, lōripedis, *bowlegged*

impiger, impigra, impigrum, *energetic, active*

dictāta, -ōrum, n. pl., *lessons, rules*

   ad dictāta, *according to the rules*

affirmō, -āre, -āvī, -ātus, *to affirm, assert*

1. Mārcus dīxit sē multōs et variōs hominēs et prīncipem in amphitheātrō vīsūrum esse.

_____

2. Mārcus dīxit paria gladiātōrum ex arēnā regressa esse.

_____

3. Mārcus dīxit Thraecēs Titō maximē fāvisse.

_____

4. Optimī gladiātōrēs ante merīdiem, bonī post merīdiem pugnant.

_____

5. Eucleidēs dīcit gladiātōrēs dēcrepitōs dē Petrōniō scrīpsisse.

_____

6. Petrōnius scrīpsit tōtam turbam spectātōrum verberātam esse.

_____

7. Cornēlia spērat sē merīdiānōs ferōcissimōs in amphitheātrō pugnantēs brevī tempore spectātūram esse.

_____

ANDROCLES AND THE LION

In addition to vocabulary, the activity in this chapter focuses on:
Aulus Gellius's story of Androcles and the lion.

Go Online
PHSchool.com
Web Code: jgd-0022

Vocabulary

Activity 49a Vocabulary

Study the vocabulary list on pages 227–228 alone or with a partner.

Androcles and the Lion

Activity 49b Reading Latin

The following is the complete story of Androcles (or Androclus, as spelled here) and the lion as told by Aulus Gellius (V. 14), a Roman scholar and writer of the second half of the second century A.D. Read the sections that are given in English translation and write your own translations of the sections that are given in Latin. Write your translations on a separate sheet or sheets of paper. You may use the vocabulary at the end of Book II in addition to the vocabulary and aids that are given with each Latin passage.

1. Apion, who was called Plistonices, was a man who had read widely and possessed an extensive and varied knowledge of things Greek. In his works, which are quite famous, is contained an account of almost all the remarkable things that are to be seen and heard in Egypt. Now, in his accounts of what he claims to have heard or read, he is perhaps too wordy and wrongly tries to show off, for he is always advertising his own learning. But, this incident that he describes in the fifth book of his *Egyptian History*, he declares that he neither heard nor read but saw himself with his own eyes in the city of Rome.

1 "In Circō Maximō," inquit, "vēnātiōnis amplissimae pugna populō dabātur. Eius
2 reī, Rōmae cum forte essem, spectātor," inquit, "fuī. Multae ibi saevientēs ferae
3 magnitūdinēs bēstiārum excellentēs omniumque invīsitāta aut fōrma erat
4 aut ferōcia. Sed praeter alia omnia leōnum," inquit, "immānitās admīrātiōnī fuit
5 praeterque omnēs cēterōs ūnus."

Name _____ Date _____ Period _____

1 **vēnātiō, vēnātiōnis**, f., *wild-beast fight*
  amplissimus, -a, -um, *very large, very impressive*
2 **saeviēns, saevientis**, *raging, savage*
  fera, -ae, f., *wild animal* (supply the verb **erant** with **ferae**)
3 **magnitūdō, magnitūdinis**, f., *size* (translate the accusative plural as singular)
  excellō, excellere, *to surpass* (the nominative participle modifies **ferae**)
  invīsitātus, -a, -um, *never seen before, unusual*
  fōrma, -ae, f., *appearance, shape*
4 **praeter**, prep. + acc., *except, beyond*
  immānitās, immānitātis, f., *huge size* (translate the genitive plural **leōnum** with **immānitās**)

2. "This one lion had attracted the attention and eyes of all because of the activity and huge size of his body, his terrific and deep roar, the development of his muscles, and the mane streaming over his shoulders."

6 "Intrōductus erat inter complūrēs cēterōs ad pugnam bēstiārum datōs servus virī
7 cōnsulāris; eī servō Androclus nōmen fuit. Hunc ille leō ubi vīdit procul, repente,"
8 inquit, "quasi admīrāns stetit ac deinde sēnsim atque placidē, tamquam nōscitābundus,
9 ad hominem accēdit."

7 **cōnsulāris, -is, -e**, *of consular rank*
  repente, adv., *suddenly*
8 **sēnsim**, adv., *gradually*
  nōscitābundus, -a, -um, *recognizing*
9 **accēdō, accēdere, accessī, accessus**, *to approach*

3. "Then, wagging his tail in a mild and caressing way, after the manner and fashion of fawning dogs, he came close to the man, who was now half dead with fright, and gently licked his feet and hands. The man Androclus, while submitting to the caresses of so fierce a beast, regained his lost courage and gradually turned his eyes to look at the lion."

10 "Tum quasi mūtuā recognitiōne factā laetōs," inquit, "et grātulābundōs vidērēs
11 hominem et leōnem."

10 **grātulābundus, -a, -um**, *offering joyful greetings*
  vidērēs, *you could see*

4. Apion says that at this sight, so truly astonishing, the people broke out into great shouts; and Gaius Caesar called Androclus to him and asked why that fiercest of lions had spared him alone. Then Androclus related a strange and surprising story. "My master," he said, "was governing Africa with proconsular authority. While there, I was forced by his undeserved and daily whippings to run away. Hoping to find hiding places safe from my master, the ruler of that country, I took refuge in lonely plains and deserts, intending, if food should fail me, to seek death in some form."

12 "Tum sōle mediō," inquit, "rabidō et flagrantī specum quandam nactus remōtam
13 latebrōsamque, in eam mē penetrō et recondō. Neque multō post ad eandem specum
14 vēnit hic leō, dēbilī ūnō et cruentō pede, gemitūs ēdēns et murmura, dolōrem
15 cruciātumque vulneris commiserantia."

> 12 **rabidus, -a, -um,** *raging, fierce*
>
> **flagrāns, flagrantis,** *blazing, scorching* (three adjectives modify **sōle**)
>
> **specus, -ūs,** f., *cave* (note the gender)
>
> **nancīscor, nancīscī, nactus sum,** *to get, find, arrive at*
>
> 13 **latebrōsus, -a, -um,** *offering a place to hide*
>
> **penetrō, -āre, -āvī, -ātus,** *to cause to go into a thing or place*
>
> > **mē penetrō,** *I enter*
>
> **recondō, recondere, recondidī, reconditus,** *to put away, hide*
>
> 14 **dēbilis, -is, -e,** *feeble, lame* (note the ablative absolute)
>
> **cruentus, -a, -um,** *bloody*
>
> **ēdō, ēdere, ēdidī, ēditus,** *to give forth*
>
> 15 **cruciātus, -ūs,** m., *torture, pain*
>
> **commiseror, -ārī, -ātus sum,** *to seek pity/sympathy for something*

5. And then, at the first sight of the approaching lion, Androclus said that his mind was overwhelmed with fear and dread. "But when the lion," he said, "had entered what was evidently his own lair and saw me cowering at a distance, he approached me mildly and gently, and lifting up his foot, was clearly showing it to me and holding it out as if to ask for help."

16 "Ibi," inquit, "ego stirpem ingentem, vēstīgiō pedis eius haerentem, revellī
17 conceptamque saniem vulnere intimō expressī accūrātiusque sine magnā iam
18 formīdine siccāvī penitus atque dētersī cruōrem. Illā tunc meā operā et medellā
19 levātus, pede in manibus meīs positō, recubuit et quiēvit atque ex eō diē
20 triennium tōtum ego et leō in eādem specū eōdemque et vīctū vīximus."

16 **vēstīgiō:** dative with **haerentem**

   vēstīgiō pedis, *the bottom of his foot, the pad of his paw*

revellō, revellere, revellī, revulsus, *to pull out*

17 **conceptus, -a, -um,** *that had been produced*

saniēs, -ēī, f., *discharge from a wound, pus*

intimus, -a, -um, *the inmost part of* (**vulnere intimō** is ablative of place

   where without a preposition; take with **conceptam**)

accūrātius, comparative of **accūrātē,** adv., *carefully*

18 **formīdō, formīdinis,** f., *fear*

siccō, -āre, -āvī, -ātus, *to dry*

penitus, adv., *from within, thoroughly*

dētergeō, dētergēre, dētersī, dētersus, *to wipe off, clean away*

cruor, cruōris, m., *blood*

tunc, adv., *then*

opera, -ae, f., *effort*

medella, -ae, f., *treatment, cure*

19 **levō, -āre, -āvī, -ātus,** *to raise up, relieve, make well*

20 **triennium, -ī,** n., *a period of three years*

vīctus, -ūs, m., *food*

6. "For he used to bring for me to the cave the choicest parts of the game that he took in hunting. Having no means of making a fire, I dried the meat in the noonday sun and ate it. But," he said, "after I had finally grown tired of that wild life, I left the cave when the lion had gone off to hunt, and after traveling nearly three days, I was seen and caught by some soldiers and taken from Africa to Rome to my master. He at once had me condemned to death by being thrown to the wild beasts. But," he said, "I see that this lion was also captured, after I left him, and that he is now repaying me for my kindness and for my curing him."

Apion records that Androclus told this story, and that when it had been made known to the people by being written out in full on a tablet and carried around the Circus, at the request of all Androclus was freed, acquitted, and presented with the lion by vote of the people.

21 "Posteā," inquit, "vidēbāmus Androclum et leōnem, lōrō tenuī revīnctum, urbe
22 tōtā circum tabernās īre, dōnārī aere Androclum, flōribus spargī leōnem, omnēs
23 ubīque obviōs dīcere: 'Hic est leō hospes hominis, hic est homō medicus leōnis.'"

21 **lōrum, -ī,** n., *leather thong, leash*

tenuis, -is, -e, *thin*

revinciō, revincīre, revīnxī, revīnctus, *to tie, bind*

22 **aes, aeris,** n., *bronze, money*

    flōs flōris, m., *flower*

    spargō, spargere, sparsī, sparsus, *to scatter, sprinkle*

23 **ubīque,** adv., *everywhere*

    obvius, -a, -um, *who comes in the way/meets*

Activity 49c Questions on the Story

Answer the following questions in brief paragraphs in English on a separate sheet of paper:

1. How credible is Apion as a storyteller? How credible is his story?

2. When Androclus first addresses Caesar, how does he seek to gain sympathy for himself?

3. What human traits does the lion exhibit?

4. How do both Androclus and the lion display sympathy for one another and generosity during their encounter and life in the cave?

5. Why did Androclus's master condemn him to death?

6. What character trait did Androclus's master lack that both the lion and Androclus possess?

7. What is the moral of the story?

NOTHING EVER HAPPENS

Go Online
PHSchool.com
Web Code: jgd-0023

In addition to vocabulary and the story, the activities in this chapter focus on:
1. the present and perfect subjunctive.
2. the imperfect and pluperfect subjunctive (review).
3. result clauses.
4. sequence of tenses.

Vocabulary

Activity 50a Vocabulary

*Study the vocabulary list on pages 229–230 alone or with a partner. Go to the corresponding
list on the Companion website where you will find a list of words anticipating result clauses.*

The Story

Activity 50b Vocabulary in Context

Fill in the blanks with Latin words to match the English cues:

1. _____ caelō _____ ita _____ ut nātūra
   ipsa gaudēre vidērētur. (sun) (clear, bright) (was shining)

2. _____ laetissimī cantābant, sed Cornēlia tamen trīstis mussābat,

   "_____ _____ solitūdinis." (Birds) (I am bored)

3. Cornēlia ab omnibus _____ _____ ut miserrima esset.
   (to such an extent) (had been ignored)

4. Mārcus Cornēliae dīxit in tablīnum eam festīnāre _____. (ought)

5. Cornēlia vultūs patris et mātris _____ sollicita fīēbat. (watching)

6. Valerius _____ Brundisiō advēnerat. (recently)

7. Valerius _____ nōbilī nātus est. (clan)

8. "Ego et pater tuus," inquit Aurēlia, "putāmus nūllum _____

   _____ esse Valeriō." (young man) (similar to, like)

9. "_____ _____," Aurēlia inquit, "patrem

   _____ fīliam, īnsciā mātre." (It is not fitting) (to betroth)

Forms

Present and Perfect Subjunctive

Activity 50c Forming Present and Perfect Subjunctives

Change each present subjunctive to perfect and each perfect subjunctive to present, keeping the same person, number, and voice:

1. mittās   _____

2. cognōscātur   (neut.)   _____

3. subsequantur   (fem.)   _____

4. exsiluerit   _____

5. velint   _____

6. spectāverimus   _____

7. habeātis   _____

8. ierit   _____

9. māluerim   _____

10. tollāmus   _____

Imperfect and Pluperfect Subjunctives: Review

Activity 50d Forming Imperfect and Pluperfect Subjunctives

Change each imperfect subjunctive to pluperfect and each pluperfect subjunctive to imperfect, keeping the same person, number, and voice:

1. inciperēs   _____

2. admīrārentur   (fem.)   _____

3. incessissem   _____

4. ostentus esset   _____

5. māllēmus   _____

6. laesae essēmus   _____

7. sēnsisset   _____

8. lāpsa essent   _____

9. tergērēris   (masc.)   _____

10. repeterem   _____

Building the Meaning

Result Clauses

Activity 50e Result Clauses and Sequence of Tenses

Fill in the blanks with Latin words to match the English cues. Use the present or imperfect subjunctive, according to the sequence of tenses. Do not use perfect subjunctives:

1. Tālis iuvenis est Valerius ut Cornēliō _____ fīliam eī dēspondēre. (it pleases)

2. Tālis iuvenis erat Valerius ut Cornēliō _____ fīliam eī dēspondēre. (it pleased)

3. Pater tam gravī vultū loquitur ut Cornēlia _____ quid acciderit. (wonders)

4. Pater tam gravī vultū locūtus est ut Cornēlia _____ quid accidisset. (wondered)

5. Cornēlia adeō perturbāta est ut vix loquī _____. (is able)

6. Cornēlia adeō perturbāta est ut submissā vōce _____. (she replies)

7. Cornēlia adeō perturbāta erat ut submissā vōce _____. (she replied)

8. Cornēlia tam laeta est ut vix loquī _____. (is able)

9. Cornēlia tam laeta erat ut vix loquī _____. (was able)

10. Cornēlia tam laeta subitō fit ut omnia Flāviae nārrāre _____. (desires)

Activity 50f Indirect Questions and Sequence of Tenses

Fill in the blanks with Latin words to match the English cues. Use the proper tense of the subjunctive according to the sequence of tenses:

1. Cornēlia nōn intellegit cūr Eucleidēs verbum nūllum sibi _____. (says)

2. Cornēlia nōn intellegit cūr Eucleidēs verbum nūllum sibi _____. (said)

3. Cornēlia nōn intellēxit cūr Eucleidēs verbum nūllum sibi _____. (was saying)

4. Cornēlia nōn intellēxit cūr Eucleidēs verbum nūllum sibi _____. (had said)

5. Cornēlia mīrābātur quid _____. (was happening)

6. Cornēlia mīrābātur quid _____. (had happened)

7. Cornēlia nōn rogat cūr pater sē Valeriō _____. (is promising)

8. Cornēlia nōn rogāvit cūr pater sē Valeriō _____. (had promised)

9. Cornēlia nōn rogāvit cūr pater sē Valeriō _____. (was promising)

10. Cornēlia nōn rogat cūr pater sē Valeriō _____. (has promised)

Applying What You Have Learned

Activity 50g Writing the Language

Translate the following English sentences into Latin. Include all long marks. Use the stories and vocabulary lists in your textbook, as well as the vocabulary lists in this book, to help you:

1. When all the relatives and friends had assembled in the atrium, Cornelius betrothed Cornelia to Valerius.

   _____

2. Cornelius replied, "I betroth (her)," so loudly (with so great a voice) that all were able to hear.

   _____

3. Sextus wonders why Valerius wants to marry Cornelia.

   _____

4. The bridegroom and bride thanked all the relatives and friends.

   _____

5. Flavia, when she congratulates Cornelia, is so happy that she cries.

   _____

Activity 50h Expanding Your English Vocabulary

Fill in the blanks. You may consult Latin and English dictionaries in doing this activity:

1. The Latin noun **coniūnx, coniugis,** m./f., means _____

   or _____. It is a compound of the prefix **con-,** meaning

   _____, and the base **iug-** or **iung-,** meaning "yoke" or "to join by yoking,"

   which is seen in the Latin words _____ and _____.

   From the Latin word **coniūnx** is derived the English word *conjugal*, which means

   _____.

2. The English word *consort* is derived from the Latin prefix **con-,** meaning

   _____, and the Latin noun **sors, sortis,** f., meaning

   _____. The English word *consort* means _____ or

   _____, and is especially used of the spouse of a _____.

3. The Latin word **uxor, uxōris,** f., means _____. The English adjective

   uxorial means _____; the English adjective *uxorious* has a pejorative

   meaning: _____.

4. The English words *dower* and *dowry* are derived through Middle English and Old French

   from the Latin word **dōs,** meaning _____. A dowry is

   _____

5. The Latin noun **marītus, -ī,** m., means _____. From it is derived the

   English word *marital*, meaning _____. Also derived from **marītus** and its

   related Latin verb **marītō, -āre,** by way of Middle English and Old French is the English

   verb _____ and the English noun _____.

6. From the Latin noun **mātrimōnium, -ī,** n., meaning _____, is derived the

   English word _____. This word is applied to the state of

   _____.

7. The Latin verb **nūbō, nūbere, nūpsī, nūptūrus** means _____. From

it are derived the English adjective *connubial*, meaning _____, and the

English noun *nuptials*, meaning _____. The English adjective *nuptial*

means _____.

8. From the Latin verb **spondeō, spondēre, spopondī, spōnsus,** meaning

_____, is derived the English word *spouse*, meaning

_____. Also derived from the Latin verb **spondeō** is the

English verb *espouse*, meaning specifically _____ and more generally

_____, as in the sentence, "He finally espoused the cause of justice."

9. Some English words having to do with marriage are derived from Old English and

Anglo-Saxon rather than Latin. Thus, *betroth*, meaning _____ or

_____ is derived from the Old English word *treowth*, meaning

_____. The English word *troth* is derived from this same Old English word

and means _____. The Old English word *wedd*, meaning "a pledge," gave

us the modern English verb _____ and the noun _____.

This noun is used to refer to the legal rather than the religious aspect of marriage.

Activity 50i Reading Latin

*Look at the new vocabulary following this story. Then read the story taken from Aulus
Gellius (X.10), and answer the questions that follow in English:*

1 Veterēs Graecōs ānulum habuisse in digitō accēpimus sinistrae manūs, quī minimō est

2 proximus. Rōmānōs quoque hominēs āiunt sīc plērumque ānulīs ūsitātōs. Causam esse

3 huius reī Apion in librīs Aegyptiacīs hanc dīcit, quod īnsectīs apertīsque hūmānīs

4 corporibus, ut mōs in Aegyptō fuit, quās Graecī anatomās appellant, repertum est nervum

5 quendam tenuissimum ab eō ūnō digitō, dē quō dīximus, ad cor hominis pergere ac

6 pervenīre; proptereā nōn īnscītum vīsum est eum potissimum digitum tālī honōre

7 decorandum, quī continēns et quasi cōnexus esse cum prīncipātū cordis vidērētur.

1 **accēpimus = audīvimus**

2 **plērumque**, adv., *generally, for the most part*

   ūsitor, -ārī, -ātus sum + abl., *to make common use of* (supply **esse** with
      ūsitātōs)

3 **Aegyptiacus, -a, -um,** *Egyptian*

   librīs Aegyptiacīs: Apion's books were on Egyptian history

   īnsecō, īnsecāre, īnsecuī, īnsectus, *to cut into*

4 **mōs, mōris,** m., *custom*

   quās = id quod

   anatoma, -ae [Greek word], f., *dissection*

   reperiō, reperīre, repperī, repertus, *to find, discover*

      repertum est: here used as an impersonal verb introducing an accusative
         and infinitive

   nervus, -ī, m., *tendon, nerve*

5 **tenuis, -is, -e,** *thin, slight, delicate*

   cor, cordis, n., *heart*

   pergō, pergere, perrēxī, perrēctūrus, *to proceed*

6 **proptereā,** adv., *therefore*

   īnscītus, -a, -um, *unreasonable*

   potissimum, adv., *especially*

   honor, honōris, m., *honor*

7 **decorandum (esse),** *ought to be honored, distinguished*

   continēns, continentis, *closely associated, linked*

   conectō, conectere, conexuī, conexus, *to join together*

   prīncipātus, -ūs, m., *leadership, preeminence*

1. On which finger and hand did the Greeks and Romans wear rings?

_____

_____

2. What does the Greek word **anatoma** mean?

_____

3. What did **anatoma** of human bodies reveal?

_____

_____

4. With what organ did this nerve connect the finger?

_____

_____

5. Why was that finger thought worthy to be the ring-finger?

_____

_____

MARCUS COMES OF AGE

In addition to vocabulary and the story, the activities in this chapter focus on: indirect commands.

Web Code: jgd-0024

Vocabulary

Activity 51a Vocabulary

Study the vocabulary lists on pages 231–232 alone or with a partner. Go to the corresponding list on the Companion website where you will find a list of words anticipating indirect commands.

The Story

Activity 51b Vocabulary in Context

Fill in the blanks with Latin words to match the English cues:

1. Cornēlius _____ propinquōs invītāverat ut apud sē convenīrent et fīlium

   suum togam _____ _____ spectārent. (some) (plain white) (assuming)

2. Iānitor clientēs rogāvit ut _____ trānsgrederentur et in ātrium intrārent. (threshold)

3. _____ nōn invītātus appropinquāvit, iānitōrem _____

   nē sē _____. (If anyone) (begged) (to send away)

4. Mārcus, ut pater eī prius _____, togam praetextam et bullam Laribus

   _____ cōnsecrāvit. (had instructed/ordered) (belonging to the household)

5. Cornēlius servō _____ ut Mārcō togam pūram trāderet. (ordered)

6. Ambō parentēs Mārcum togā novā indūtum _____. (embraced)

7. Patre et propinquīs et amīcīs et clientibus _____, Mārcus Tabulāriō
   appropinquāvit. (accompanying)

8. Nōmine in tabulīs pūblicīs īnscrīptō, Mārcus propter tantam ergā sē

   _____ omnibus _____.
   (kindness) (thanked)

Building the Meaning

Indirect Commands

Activity 51c Indirect Commands

Complete the indirect commands in the following sentences by supplying the correct form of the verb in parentheses. In each pair of sentences, the subordinate clause is first in primary and then in secondary sequence:

1. a. Cornēlius amīcōs clientēsque invītat ut ad domum suam crās _____.
(venīre)

    b. Cornēlius amīcōs clientēsque invītāvit ut ad domum suam crās _____.
(venīre)

2. a. Iānitor aliōs domuī appropinquantēs rogat ut in domum Cornēliī _____
(prōcēdere)

    b. Iānitor aliōs domuī appropinquantēs rogāvit ut in domum Cornēliī _____
(prōcēdere)

3. a. Iānitor aliīs domuī appropinquantibus praecipit ut in viā _____. (manēre)

    b. Iānitor aliīs domuī appropinquantibus praecipiēbat ut in viā _____.
(manēre)

4. a. Hī iānitōrem ōrant nē sē _____. (dīmittere)

    b. Hī iānitōrem ōrāvērunt nē sē _____. (dīmittere)

5. a. Iānitor eīs imperat ut statim _____. (discēdere)

    b. Iānitor eīs imperāvit ut statim _____. (discēdere)

6. a. Iānitor omnēs domum intrantēs rogat ut in ātrium _____. (prōgredī)

    b. Iānitor omnēs domum intrantēs rogāvit ut in ātrium _____. (prōgredī)

7. a. Cornēlius servō imperat ut togam pūram Mārcō _____. (induere)

    b. Cornēlius servō imperāvit ut togam pūram Mārcō _____. (induere)

8. a. Cornēlius eōs quī sē comitantur rogat ut extrā Tabulārium _____. (manēre)

    b. Cornēlius eōs quī sē comitābantur rogāvit ut extrā Tabulārium _____.
(manēre)

9. a. Cornēlius multōs invītat ut apud sē hodiē _____. (cēnāre)

    b. Cornēlius multōs invītāvit ut apud sē hodiē _____. (cēnāre)

Activity 51d Indirect Commands

Underline the indirect commands in the following sentences and translate the sentences into English:

1. Cum nōmen Mārcī in tabulīs īnscrīptum esset, eōs quī extrā Tabulārium manēbant Cornēlius invītāvit ut ad domum suam redīrent.

   _____

2. Cornēlius praecēpit ut omnēs clientēs in domum ingrederentur.

   _____

   _____

3. Illōs quī nōn invitātī sunt iānitor monet ut abeant.

   _____

4. Illī tamen ōrānt ut sibi in viā manēre liceat.

   _____

5. Canēs Apollodōrī caupōnis Cornēlia hortābatur ut pilam repeterent.

   _____

   _____

6. Pseudolus laniō persuāsit ut leporem grātīs cum porcō ēmptō sibi daret.

   _____

   _____

7. Aurēlia tamen Pseudolō imperāvit ut sibi leporem trāderet et ad vīllam regrederētur.

   _____

   _____

8. Dāvus aliōs servōs rogāverat ut sibi dīcerent ubi Geta esset, sed frustrā.

   _____

   _____

Name _____ Date _____ Period _____

9. Itaque Davus servīs imperāvit ut Getam canibus peterent.

_____

10. Sextus Eucleidem obsecrāvit nē cum Cornēliō dē suīs in lūdō factīs loquerētur.

_____

_____

11. Prīnceps, quī senātum cōnsulere volēbat, imperāvit ut omnēs senātōrēs statim Rōmam redīrent.

_____

_____

Applying What You Have Learned

Activity 51e Writing the Language

Translate the following English sentences into Latin. Include all long marks. Use the stories and vocabulary lists in your textbook, as well as the vocabulary lists in this book, to help you:

1. Aurelia persuaded Cornelius to invite all his clients.

_____

2. Aurelia instructs the cook to prepare a very good dinner.

_____

3. Sextus, since he wished to see the ceremony, begged Cornelius not to send him (**sē**) away to his bedroom.

_____

4. Cornelius begged those invited to become silent.

_____

5. Cornelius urged all to return to his house and to dine with him.

_____

© Pearson Education, Inc., or its affiliates. All rights reserved.

Activity 51f Expanding Your English Vocabulary

For each italicized English word below, give the Latin word to which the English word is related. Then complete each sentence by filling in a word at the right. Finally, give the meaning of each Latin word you write at the left:

Latin Word
Meaning of the Latin Word

If you ...

1. _____ *purify* something, you make it _____
   _____

2. _____ receive a *subliminal* message, _____
   _____ you receive a message which
   is below the _____ of your
   conscious perception.

3. _____ issue an *imperative*, you give an _____
   _____

4. _____ *dismiss* someone, you _____ _____
   _____ the person.

5. _____ refer to a *precept*, you refer to
   _____ a rule or _____

6. _____ show *benevolence* toward
   _____ someone, you show _____ _____
   toward the person.

7. _____ *eliminate* something, you exclude
   _____ it by putting it (figuratively
   speaking) outside the _____

8. _____ fear the *concomitant* danger of
   _____ mountain climbing, you fear
   the danger that _____ it. _____

9. _____ remove *impurities* from water, you
   _____ remove those substances that
   prevent the water from being _____

10. _____ express your *gratitude* to
    _____ someone, you give them your _____

Activity 51g Reading Latin

Look at the new vocabulary following this story. Then read the story and answer the questions that follow with complete Latin sentences:

Ambrosius Theodosius Macrobius was a Roman grammarian and philosopher who wrote under the reigns of Honorius and Arcadius (A.D. 395–A.D. 423). In his work, *Saturnalia* I.6.8–9, Macrobius explains the origin of boys wearing the **bulla** and the **toga praetexta**:

1 Tarquinius Prīscus, rēx quīntus ā Rōmulō, dē Sabīnīs ēgit triumphum: quō bellō fīlium suum
2 annōs quattuordecim nātum, quod hostem manū percusserat, et prō cōntiōne laudāvit et
3 bullā aureā praetextāque dōnāvit, īnsigniēns puerum ultrā annōs fortem praemiīs virīlitātis et
4 honōris. Nam sīcut praetexta magistrātuum, ita bulla gestāmen erat triumphantium, quam in
5 triumphō prae sē gerēbant inclūsīs intrā remediīs quae crēderent adversus invidiam
6 valentissima.

    1 **Sabīnī, -ōrum**, m. pl., *the Sabines (a neighboring tribe)*
      triumphus, -ī, m., *triumph*
        ēgit triumphum: *held a triumph*

    2 **hostis, hostis**, gen. pl., **hostium**, m./f., *enemy*
      percutiō, percutere, percussī, percussus, *to strike, kill*
      prō, prep. + abl., *in front of*
      cōntiō, cōntiōnis, f., *assembly*

    3 **praetextā = togā praetextā**
      dōnō, -āre, -āvī, -ātus, *to present X (acc.) with Y (abl.)*
      īnsigniō, īnsignīre, *to mark, distinguish*
      ultrā, prep. + acc., *beyond*
      praemium, -ī, n., *reward*
      virīlitās, virīlitātis, f., *manliness, courage*

    4 **sīcut**, adv., *just as*
      magistrātus, -ūs, m., *civil office; public officer*
      gestāmen, gestāminis, n., *ornament*
      triumphō, -āre, -āvī, -ātus, *to triumph, hold a triumph*

    5 **prae**, prep. + acc., *before, in front of*
      inclūdō, inclūdere, inclūsī, inclūsus, *to enclose*
      intrā, adv., *inside (The bulla was a hollow locket.)*
      remedium, -ī, n., *remedy, antidote, talisman*
      adversus, prep. + acc., *against*
      invidia, -ae f., *jealousy (The Romans feared that a triumphing general might be so proud that he might incur the jealousy of the gods.)*

    6 **valēns, valentis**, *strong, powerful*

1. What did King Tarquin's son do in the war against the Sabines?

_____

2. What three rewards did he give his son?

_____

3. Who else wore the **toga praetexta**? The **bulla**?

_____

4. What did the **bulla** enclose?

_____

PAPIRIUS PRAETEXTATUS

Web Code: jgd-0025

In addition to vocabulary and the story, the activities in this chapter focus on:
1. impersonal verbs.
2. the story of Papirius Praetextatus as told by Aulus Gellius.

Vocabulary

Activity 52a Vocabulary

Study the vocabulary list on page 233 alone or with a partner. Go to the corresponding list on the Companion website where you will find a list of impersonal verbs.

Building the Meaning

Impersonal Verbs

Activity 52b Sentences with Impersonal Verbs

Translate the "a" sentences in each pair into English. Note the construction of the sentence with the impersonal verb. Then translate the "b" sentences into Latin:

1. a. Cornēliam urbis taedet. Ad vīllam rūsticam regredī vult.

_____

_____

b. Flavia is bored with the country house and farm. She wants to go to Rome.

_____

2. a. Quod Cornēlius fīliam in tablīnō statim adesse iussit, Cornēliam festīnāre oportet.

_____

_____

b. Flavia and Vinia ought to go to Rome immediately, for Vinia will be the bride's attendant.

_____

3. a. Cornēlius Cornēliam rogat: "Placetne tibi Valerium tē in mātrimōnium dūcere?"

_____

b. Vinia asks: "Does it please you to remain in Rome, Flavia?"

_____

4. a. Decet spōnsum ānulum aureum tertiō digitō sinistrae manūs spōnsae aptāre.

_____

_____

b. It is proper that the groom should also give (his) bride a kiss.

_____

5. a. Flāvia laetissima rogat, "Licetne mihi Rōmae manēre?"

_____

b. "You may, if it pleases (you)," says (her) mother.

_____

Activity 52c Reading Latin

The following is the complete and unadapted story of Papirius Praetextatus as told by the Roman author Aulus Gellius (I.23). Write translations of each of the sections. You may use the vocabulary at the back of your textbook in addition to the vocabulary and aids that are given with each Latin passage. Write your translations on a separate sheet or sheets of paper.

1.

1 Mōs anteā senātōribus Rōmae fuit in Cūriam cum praetextātīs fīliīs introīre.
2 Tum, cum in senātū rēs maior quaepiam cōnsultāta eaque in diem posterum
3 prōlāta est placuitque ut eam rem super quā tractāvissent nē quis ēnūntiāret
4 priusquam dēcrēta esset, māter Papiriī puerī, quī cum parente suō in Cūriā
5 fuerat, percontāta est fīlium quidnam in senātū patrēs ēgissent.

    2 **quispiam, quaepiam, quodpiam,** *some, a certain*
        cōnsultō, -āre, -āvī, -ātus, *to discuss* (with **cōnsultāta,** supply **erat**)
    3 **ut...nē quis,** *that no one*

    super, prep. + abl., *about, concerning*

    tractō, -āre, -āvī, -ātus, *to handle,* *deal with; to carry on a discussion, deliberate*

4 **priusquam,** conj., *before*

    dēcernō, dēcernere, dēcrēvī, dēcrētus, *to settle, decide*

5 **percontor, -ārī, -ātus sum,** *to question, ask*

    quisnam, quaenam, quidnam, *exactly who, exactly what* (often introducing
        direct or indirect questions)

2.

6 Puer respondit tacendum esse neque id dīcī licēre. Mulier fit audiendī cupidior;

7 sēcrētum reī et silentium puerī animum eius ad inquīrendum ēverberat; quaerit

8 igitur compressius violentiusque. Tum puer, mātre urgente, lepidī atque fēstīvī

9 mendāciī cōnsilium capit.

    6 **tacendum esse,** *that it must be keep quiet*

      audiendī, *of hearing*

      cupidus, -a, -um + gen., *desirous (of)*

    7 **sēcrētum, -ī,** n., *secret*

      inquīrō, inquīrere, inquīsīvī, inquīsītus, *to inquire*

         ad inquīrendum, *for asking, to asking*

      ēverberō, -āre, -āvī, -ātus, *to beat, stir up*

    8 **compressius,** comparative of **compressē,** adv., *forcefully, urgently*

      violentius, comparative of **violenter,** adv., *violently, forcefully*

      lepidus, -a, -um, *charming, clever*

      fēstīvus, -a, -um, *festive, witty*

    9 **mendācium, -ī,** n., *falsehood*

3.

10 Āctum in senātū dīxit utrum vidērētur ūtilius exque rē pūblicā esse ūnusne

11 ut duās uxōrēs habēret an ut ūna apud duōs nūpta esset. Hoc illa ubi audīvit,

12 animus compavēscit, domō trepidāns ēgreditur, ad cēterās mātrōnās perfert.

    10 **Āctum:** supply **esse**

       ūtilis, -is, -e, *useful*

       ex, prep. + abl., here, *in accord with, in the interests of*

       rēs pūblica, reī pūblicae, f., *the state, the public good*

       -ne . . . an: these particles correlate the two parts of the double question; do
          not translate **-ne; an** = *or*

    11 **ut,** delayed conjunction; translate before **ūnusne**

       nūbō, nūbere, nūpsī, nūptus, *to marry*

    12 **compavēscō, compavēscere,** *to become fearful*

4.

13 Vēnit ad senātum postrīdiē mātrum familiās caterva. Lacrimantēs atque

14 obsecrantēs ōrant ūna potius ut duōbus nūpta fieret quam ut ūnī duae.

15 Senātōrēs, ingredientēs in Cūriam, quae illa mulierum intemperiēs et quid sibi

16 postulātiō istaec vellet, mīrābantur.

> 13 **māter familiās, mātris familiās,** f., *mistress of a household, matron* (**familiās**
>   is an old, archaic genitive singular of **familia**)
>
> 14 **ut,** delayed conjunction; translate before **ūna**
>   **nūpta** + dat., *married (to)*
>
> 15 **intemperiēs, intemperiēī,** f., *intemperate/outrageous behavior*
>
> 16 **postulātiō, postulātiōnis,** f., *request, demand*
>   **istaec:** an emphatic **ista**
>   **volō,** here, *to mean* (used in this sense with **sibi,** *for itself,* which need not be
>   translated). The direct objects of **vellet** are the interrogative pronouns
>   **quae,** *what things,* and **quid,** *what.* The indirect questions depend on
>   **mīrābantur,** *they were wondering.*

5.

17 Puer Papirius in medium Cūriae prōgressus, quid māter audīre īnstitisset, quid

18 ipse mātrī dīxisset, rem, sīcut fuerat, dēnārrat. Senātus fidem atque ingenium

19 puerī exōsculātur, cōnsultum facit utī posthāc puerī cum patribus in Cūriam

20 nē introeant, praeter ille ūnus Papirius, atque puerō posteā cognōmentum

21 honōris grātiā inditum "Praetextātus" ob tacendī loquendīque in aetāte

22 praetextae prūdentiam.

> 17 **īnstō, īnstāre, īnstitī** + infin., *to insist on*
>
> 18 **sīcut,** adv., *just as*
>
> 19 **exōsculor, -ārī, -ātus sum,** *to kiss; to express great admiration for*
>   **utī** = **ut**. Note **utī . . . nē** = **nē,** *that . . . not*
>   **posthāc,** adv., *after this, henceforth*
>
> 20 **praeter,** adv., *except*
>   **cognōmentum** = **cognōmen**
>
> 21 **grātiā** + preceding gen., *for the sake of, as*
>   **indō, indere, indidī, inditus,** *to give, bestow* (with **inditum** supply **est**)
>   **ob,** prep. + acc, *on account of, as a reward for*
>   **tacendī loquendīque,** *of keeping quiet and of speaking* (the genitives depend on
>   **prūdentiam,** *wisdom*)
>   **aetās, aetātis,** f., *age, time of life*

Activity 52d Reading Comprehension

Answer the following questions in English on a separate sheet or sheets of paper:

1. What words in the second passage tell us the most about the character and personality of Papirius's mother? What kind of person is she?

2. Papirius tells his mother a downright lie. How, in the second passage, does the narrator try to put a good face on this action?

3. What words in the third and fourth passages show the feelings and emotions of Papirius's mother and of the other women? What one word best characterizes the women's behavior? What sort of bias does the use of this word reveal in the men of the day or in the narrator?

4. What one verb in the fifth passage best characterizes the senators' feelings about Papirius?

5. What three qualities of character or personality do the senators admire in Papirius? Cite the three Latin nouns that express these qualities.

6. Was Papirius's mother wrong to insist so vehemently that her own son tell her the secret? Was Papirius right to tell his mother a lie?

7. How are the roles and character of the women in this story distinguished from those of the men?

8. The author of this story describes it as **iūcunda**, *entertaining*. Is there anything more to the story than mere entertainment? If so, what?

CORNELIA'S WEDDING

> *In addition to vocabulary and the story, the activities in this chapter focus on:*
> 1. purpose clauses.
> 2. the story of Arria and her ill husband as told by Pliny the Younger.

Go Online
PHSchool.com
Web Code: jgd-0026

Vocabulary

Activity 53a Vocabulary

Study the vocabulary lists on pages 234–236 alone or with a partner.

The Story

Activity 53b Vocabulary in Context

Fill in the blanks with Latin words to match the English cues:

1. Corōnae _____ _____ dōmum Cornēliōrum

   _____. (of myrtle) (and of laurel) (were decorating)

2. _____ _____ parātīs, prōnuba ad

   _____ stābat ut _____ spōnsī et novae nūptae

   _____. (sacrifices) (properly) (altar) (right hands) (to join)

3. Puerīs taedās _____ ferentibus, spōnsus et nova nūpta ad domum novam
   prōcessērunt. (burning)

4. Propinquī et amīcī _____ plēnī erant. (of good humor)

5. Valerius Cornēliam magnā cum cūrā sustulit super līmen _____.
   (so that she wouldn't stumble)

Building the Meaning

Purpose Clauses

Activity 53c Purpose Clauses

Complete the purpose clauses in the following sentences by supplying the correct form of the verb that is given in its infinitive form in parentheses:

1. a. Flāvia Rōmam venit ut Cornēliam _____. (adiuvāre)

   b. Flāvia Rōmam vēnit ut Cornēliam _____. (adiuvāre)

2. a. Ancillae hūc illūc concursant ut omnia _____. (parāre)

   b. Ancillae hūc illūc concursābant ut omnia _____. (parāre)

3. a. Multī amīcī conveniunt ut novae nūptae _____. (grātulārī)

   b. Multī amīcī convēnērunt ut novae nūptae _____. (grātulārī)

4. a. Iānitor baculum habet ut eōs quī neque amīcī neque propinquī sint

     _____. (repellere)

   b. Iānitor baculum habuit ut eōs quī neque amīcī neque propinquī essent

     _____. (repellere)

5. a. Ancilla in cubiculum festīnat ut Cornēliae speculum _____. (dare)

   b. Ancilla in cubiculum festīnāvit ut Cornēliae speculum _____. (dare)

6. a. Omnēs conticēscunt nē quis ōmen malum _____. (dīcere)

   b. Omnēs conticuērunt nē quis ōmen malum _____. (dīcere)

7. a. Auspex prōcēdit ut porcum _____. (sacrificāre)

   b. Auspex prōcessit ut porcum _____. (sacrificāre)

8. a. Auspex prōcēdit ut exta _____. (īnspicere)

   b. Auspex prōcessit ut exta _____. (īnspicere)

9. a. Novae nūptae cavēre dēbent nē _____. (cadere)

   b. Novae nūptae cavēre dēbēbant nē _____. (cadere)

10. a. Nova nūpta super līmen tollitur nē _____. (lābī)

   b. Nova nūpta super līmen sublāta est nē _____. (lābī)

Activity 53d Reading Latin

The following is the story of Arria and her ill husband as told by Pliny (Letters III.16).
Write translations of both sections below. You may use the vocabulary at the back of your
textbook in addition to the vocabulary and aids that are given with each Latin passage below.
Write your translations on a separate sheet or sheets of paper.

1.

1 Aegrōtābāt Caecina Paetus, marītus Arriae, aegrōtābat et fīlius, uterque mortiferē, ut
2 vidēbātur. Fīlius dēcessit eximiā pulchritūdine parī verēcundiā, et parentibus nōn minus ob
3 alia cārus quam quod fīlius erat. Huic illa ita fūnus parāvit, ita dūxit exsequiās, ut
4 ignōrāret marītus; quīn immō quotiēns cubiculum eius intrāret, vīvere fīlium atque etiam
5 commodiōrem esse simulābat, ac persaepe interrogantī quid ageret puer, respondēbat,
6 "Bene quiēvit, libenter cibum sūmpsit."

2 **pār, paris,** *equal*

verēcundia, -ae, f., *modesty*

eximiā pulchritūdine parī verēcundiā: two descriptive ablative phrases
with the connective **et** omitted (asyndeton)

ob, prep. + acc., *on account of*

4 **quīn immō,** adv., *indeed*

quotiēns, conj. + subjunctive, *as often as, whenever*

5 **commodus, -a, -um,** *in good health*

persaepe, adv., *very often*

2.

7 Deinde, cum diū cohibitae lacrimae vincerent prōrumperentque, ēgrediēbātur; tunc sē
8 dolōrī dabat; satiāta siccīs oculīs compositō vultū redībat, tamquam orbitātem
9 forīs relīquisset. Abdidit lacrimās, operuit lūctum, āmissōque fīliō mātrem adhūc agēbat.

7 **cohibeō, -ēre, -uī, -itus,** *to hold back, restrain*

tunc, adv., *then*

8 **satiō, -āre, -āvī, -ātus,** *to satisfy, satiate*

satiāta: i.e., when she had had her fill of weeping and grief

siccīs oculīs compositō vultū: ablative absolutes; note the asyndeton and
compare **eximiā pulchritūdine parī verēcundiā** above, line 2

orbitās, orbitātis, f., *loss (of a child)*

9 **forīs,** adv., *outside the door*

abdō, abdere, abdidī, abditus, *to put away, hide*

lūctus, -ūs, m., *grief, mourning*

āmittō, āmittere, āmīsī, āmissus, *to lose*

mātrem adhūc agēbat, *she still acted (the part of) a mother*

Activity 53e Essay on the Story

On a separate sheet of paper, write an essay in which you describe the character of Arria as revealed in the passages in Activity 53d, and contrast Arria's character with that of the mother of Papirius and the other women in the passages in Activity 52c.

A SAD OCCASION

Web Code: jgd-0027

In addition to vocabulary, the activities in this chapter focus on:
a letter of Pliny the Younger on the death of Minicia Marcella.

Vocabulary

Activity 54a Vocabulary

Study the vocabulary list on pages 237–239 alone or with a partner.

Activity 54b Reading Latin

The following is a letter written by Pliny the Younger (V.16) to a friend concerning the recent death of the daughter of a mutual friend. Write translations of each of the sections. You may use the vocabulary at the back of your textbook in addition to the vocabulary and aids that are given with each Latin passage. Write your translations on a separate sheet or sheets of paper.

1. C. PLINIUS AEFULANO MARCELLINO SUO S.

1 Trīstissimus haec tibi scrībō, Fundānī nostrī fīliā minōre dēfūnctā. Quā puellā nihil

2 umquam fēstīvius amābilius, nec modo longiōre vītā sed prope immortālitāte dignius vīdī.

    1 **Fundānus -ī,** m., *Gaius Minicius Fundanus* (a close friend of Pliny and consul
        in A.D. 107)

       fīliā: her name was Minicia Marcella

       minor, minor, minus, gen., **minōris,** *smaller, younger*

       dēfungor, dēfungī, dēfūnctus sum, *to die*

    2 **fēstīvus, -a, -um,** *festal, congenial, happy*

       amābilis, -is, -e, *lovable, delightful*

         Note the lack of a connective (**et**) between the two adjectives (asyndeton).

       nec modo...sed prope, *and not only...but almost....*

       dignus, -a, -um + abl., *worthy of*

2.

3 Nōndum annōs XIIII implēverat, et iam illī anīlis prūdentia, mātrōnālis gravitās erat et

4 tamen suāvitās puellāris cum virginālī verēcundiā. Ut illa patris cervīcibus inhaerēbat! Ut

5 nōs amīcōs paternōs et amanter et modestē complectēbātur! Ut nūtrīcēs, ut paedagōgōs, ut

6 praeceptōrēs prō suō quemque officiō dīligēbat! Quam studiōsē, quam intellegenter

7 lectitābat! Ut parcē custōdītēque lūdēbat!

3   **annōs XIIII**: the girl's actual funerary urn and inscription were found
    outside Rome; the inscription gives her age as 12 (almost 13) years:
    D(īs) M(ānibus) Miniciae Marcellae Fundānī f(īliae). V(īxit)
    a(nnōs) XII m(ēnsēs) XI d(iēs) VII.

impleō, implēre, implēvī, implētus, *to fill* (used with **annōs** to express a
    person's age)

illī: dative of possession (*there was for her = she had*)

anīlis, -is, -e, *belonging to/characteristic of an old woman* (**anus, -ūs**, f.)

4   **verēcundia, -ae,** f. *modesty*

Ut...! *How...!*

cervīx, cervīcis, f., *neck* (plural for singular)

inhaereō, inhaerēre, inhaesī, inhaesūrus + dat., *to cling to*

5   **modestē,** adv., *modestly*

complector, complectī, complexus sum, *to embrace*

nūtrīx, nūtrīcis, f., *nurse* (of a child), *wet-nurse*

6   **praeceptor, praeceptōris,** m., *teacher, tutor* (here perhaps of private tutors,
    as Pliny remarks of a boy in another letter: **praeceptōrēs domī habuit**)

prō, prep. + abl., *according to*

suō, *his/her own*

quemque, *each*

studiōsē, adv., *eagerly*

intellegenter, adv., *intelligently*

7   **lectitō, -āre, -āvī, -ātus,** *to read frequently/repeatedly, to be in the habit of
    reading*

parcē, adv., *moderately, carefully*

custōdītē, adv., *cautiously*

3.

8   Quā illa temperantiā, quā patientiā, quā etiam cōnstantiā novissimam

9   valētūdinem tulit! Medicīs obsequēbātur, sorōrem patrem adhortābātur ipsamque

10 sē dēstitūtam corporis vīribus vigōre animī sustinēbat. Dūrāvit hic illī usque ad

11 extrēmum, nec aut spatiō valētūdinis aut metū mortis īnfrāctus est, quō plūrēs

12 graviōrēsque nōbīs causās relinqueret et dēsīderiī et dolōris.

8   **Quā...!** *(With) what...!*

temperantia, -ae, f., *self-control*

cōnstantia, -ae, f., *firmness, resolution*

novissimam, *newest*, i.e., *last, most recent*

9   **obsequor, obsequī, obsecūtus sum** + dat., *to follow* (a person's instructions)

10 **dēstitūtus, -a, -um** + abl., *deprived of*

    sustineō, sustinēre, sustinuī, sustentus, *to support, sustain*

    dūrō, -āre, -āvī, -ātus, *to last, remain*

    hic: i.e., her **vigor animī**

    usque ad + acc., *right up to*

11 **extrēmum, -ī,** n., *end*

    spatium, -ī, n., *length*

    īnfringō, īnfringere, īnfrēgī, īnfrāctus, *to weaken, break, crush*

    quō = ut, here introducing a result clause containing comparative adjectives

12 **dēsīderium, -ī,** n., *longing, desire* (as for a dead person)

4.

13 Ō trīste plānē acerbumque fūnus! Ō morte ipsā mortis tempus indignius! Iam
14 dēstināta erat ēgregiō iuvenī, iam ēlēctus nūptiārum diēs, iam nōs vocātī. Quod
15 gaudium quō maerōre mūtātum est! Nōn possum exprimere verbīs quantum
16 animō vulnus accēperim, cum audīvī Fundānum ipsum, ut multa lūctuōsa dolor
17 invēnit, praecipientem, quod in vestēs margarīta gemmās fuerat ērogātūrus, hoc
18 in tūs et unguenta et odōrēs impenderētur.

13 **plānē,** adv., *plainly, utterly, absolutely*

    acerbus, -a, -um, *bitter, distressing, untimely, premature* (of death)

    indignus, -a, -um, *unworthy, cruel, shocking*

14 **dēstinō, -āre, -āvī, -ātus,** *to destine, engage* (by formal arrangement). Girls
      could be promised and given in marriage as young as 12 years of age.

    ēgregius, -a, -um, *outstanding, excellent*

    ēligō, ēligere, ēlēgī, ēlēctus, *to select, choose*

15 **gaudium, -ī,** n., *joy*

    maeror, maerōris, m., *grief, sorrow, mourning*

    mūtō, -āre, -āvī, -ātus + acc. and abl., *to exchange* (one thing, acc.)
      for (another, abl.)

16 **ut multa...dolor invēnit!** *as (his) grief found many...*

    lūctuōsus, -a, -um, *sorrowful, mournful*

17 **praecipientem,** *instructing, ordering* (introducing an indirect command with
      its verb, **impenderētur,** in the subjunctive but with the usual **ut** omitted)

    quod, *that (money) which*

    margarītum, -ī, n., *pearl*

    gemma, -ae, f., *gem*

      vestēs margarīta gemmās: asyndeton

    ērogō, -āre, -āvī, -ātus, *to pay*

18   **tūs, tūris,** n., *frankincense* (used in funeral ceremonies)

      odor, odōris, m., *perfume* (used in funeral ceremonies)

      impendō, impendere, impendī, impēnsus, *to spend*

5.

19   Est quidem ille ērudītus et sapiēns, ut quī sē ab ineunte aetāte altiōribus studiīs
20   artibusque dēdiderit; sed nunc omnia, quae audiit saepe quae dīxit, aspernātur
21   expulsīsque virtūtibus aliīs pietātis est tōtus. Ignōscēs, laudābis etiam, sī cōgitāveris
22   quid āmīserit.

19   **sapiēns, sapientis,** *wise, philosophical.* This was the term for a Stoic
      philosopher, "sage," or "wise man." The Stoic school of philosophy taught
      that the "wise man" would always be in full control of his emotions.
      Minicius may have attended the philosophical school of the famous Stoic
      philosopher Musonius Rufus.

     ut quī + subjunctive; a relative clause with the subjunctive is used to describe
      a characteristic of the antecedent: *he is...wise,* (someone) *who*
      (characteristically) *has devoted himself to....* The addition of **ut** emphasizes
      cause: *since* (he is the sort of person) *who has devoted himself to....* **Ut quī**
      may thus be translated simply *since he....*

     aetās, aetātis, f., *age*

      ab ineunte aetāte, *from earliest youth*

20   **ars, artis,** gen. pl., **artium,** f., *skill, art;* pl., *liberal arts*

     dēdō, dēdere, dēdidī, dēditus + dat, *to devote* (oneself) *to.*

     audiit = audīvit

     saepe: understand with both **audiit** and **dīxit.** Note the lack of
      connective (asyndeton) between the two relative clauses.

     aspernor, -ārī, -ātus sum, *to reject*

21   **virtūs, virtūtis,** f, *virtue, moral excellence.* Here the word may refer to the
      qualities of moral character such as resolution and control over emotions
      that were taught by the Stoic philosophers.

     pietās, pietātis, f.: this word and the concept it embodies defy simple
      translation into English. **Pietās** was an attitude of respect toward others;
      here it is used of the respect, love, and compassion felt by the father for
      his daughter.

     tōtus, -a, -um + gen., *totally given over to*

     ignōscō, ignōscere, ignōvī, ignōtus + dat., *to pardon* (supply **eī,** *him*)

     cōgitāveris: future perfect, but translate as present

22   **āmittō, āmittere, āmīsī, āmissus,** *to lose*

6.

23 Āmīsit enim fīliam, quae nōn minus mōrēs eius quam ōs vultumque referēbat, tōtumque
24 patrem mīrā similitūdine exscrīpserat. Proinde sī quās ad eum dē dolōre tam iūstō litterās
25 mittēs, mementō adhibēre sōlācium nōn quasi castīgātōrium et nimis forte, sed molle et
26 hūmānum.

> 24 **exscrībō, exscrībere, exscrīpsī, exscrīptus,** *to copy, resemble*
> **proinde** (pronounce as two syllables), adv., *accordingly*
> **quās = aliquās,** *any*
> **iūstus, -a, -um,** *lawful, legitimate, appropriate*
>
> 25 **mementō** (imperative), *remember*
> **adhibeō, adhibēre, adhibuī, adhibitus,** *to provide, offer*
> **sōlācium, -ī, n.,** *consolation*
> **castīgātōrius, -a, -um,** *full of criticism/reproof*
> **nimis forte,** *too strong/severe*
> **mollis, -is, -e,** *soft, gentle*

7.

27 Quod ut facilius admittat, multum faciet mediī temporis spatium. Ut enim crūdum adhūc
28 vulnus medentium manūs reformidat, deinde patitur atque ultrō requīrit, sīc recēns animī
29 dolor cōnsōlātiōnēs rēicit ac refugit, mox dēsīderat et clēmenter admōtīs adquiēscit. Valē.

> 27 **quod:** i.e, the **sōlācium** contained in the letter that Aefulanus may send to
> Minicius
> **ut...admittat:** this clause, expressing result, functions as the object of the
> verb **faciet** in the main clause: *will bring it about that...*
> **admittō, admittere, admīsī, admissus,** *to receive, accept*
> **spatium, -ī, n.,** *space, length*
> **ut,** adv., *as*
> **crūdus, -a, -um,** *raw*
>
> 28 **medēns, medentis,** gen. pl., **medentium,** m., *doctor*
> **reformidō, -āre, -āvī, -ātus,** *to shrink back/recoil in fear from something*
> **ultrō,** adv., *voluntarily*
> **requīrō, requīrere, requīsīvī, requīsītus,** *to seek*
> **recēns, recentis,** *recent, fresh*
>
> 29 **rēiciō, rēicere, rēiēcī, rēiectus,** *to refuse to accept; to reject*
> **refugiō, refugere, refūgī,** *to shrink away from, shun, avoid*

> **admoveō, admovēre, admōvī, admōtus,** *to bring, offer.* With **admōtīs**
> supply the noun **cōnsōlātiōnibus.** The participle **admōtīs** has a
> conditional force: *if offered.*
>
> **adquiēscō, adquiēscere, adquiēvī** + dat., *to find rest/relief in something*

Activity 54c Reading Comprehension

Answer the following questions on the preceding letter in English on a separate sheet or sheets of paper:

1. In passage 1, locate an example of hyperbole (exaggeration for rhetorical effect). How is the hyperbole here appropriate to the tone and purpose of this letter?

2. What characteristics of Minicia does Pliny find most remarkable in passage 2?

3. What is the rhetorical effect of the exclamations in passage 2?

4. Locate an example of asyndeton in passage 3.

5. Why has Minicia left "more and deeper causes of longing and grief" (passage 3)? What was it about her behavior that caused even greater longing and grief?

6. What further reason for sorrow is referred to in passage 4?

7. How does the metaphorical use of the word **vulnus** in passage 4 help Pliny express what he claims "not to be able to express in words"?

8. In passage 4, the phrase **in vestēs margarīta gemmās** is balanced by the phrase **in tūs et unguenta et odōrēs.** Can you think of any explanation of why Pliny uses asyndeton in the former list and not in the latter?

9. What hints about the advanced education of Minicius are we given in passage 5? How does the education he has received differ from that received by his daughter (passage 2)?

10. What might be regarded as blameworthy in Minicius's behavior (passage 5)? How does Pliny defend him?

11. In passage 6, Pliny remarks on the similarity in character of daughter and father. What earlier indications are there in the letter that their characters were similar?

12. What will be necessary before Minicius will be able to accept even consolation that is gentle and humane (passage 7)?

13. Explain as fully as possible the comparison Pliny draws between a wound and grief (passage 7).

VOCABULARY LISTED BY PART OF SPEECH

By covering the words in one column or the other with a piece of paper with a notch in the top, test your knowledge of these words. For words in boldface, you should be able to give the English for the Latin, the Latin for the English, and all information about the Latin word as given in the entry. Practice until you can do this with no mistakes. For words not in boldface, you only need to be able to give the English for the Latin.

Chapter 28

NOUNS:

1st Declension:
neglegentia, -ae, f. — *carelessness*
sella, -ae, f. — *sedan chair*

2nd Declension:
porcus, -ī, m. — *pig*
speculum, -ī, n. — *mirror*

3rd Declension:
crīnēs, crīnium, m. pl. — *hair*
glīs, glīris, gen. pl., **glīrium,** m. — *dormouse*

ADJECTIVES:

1st and 2nd Declension:
pulcher, pulchra, pulchrum — *beautiful, pretty, handsome*
vexātus, -a, -um — *annoyed*

3rd Declension:
neglegēns, neglegentis — *careless*

RELATIVE PRONOUN:
quī, quae, quod — *who, which, that*

ADVERB:
neglegenter — *carelessly*

VERBS:

1st Conjugation:
invītō, -āre, -āvī, -ātus — *to invite*

3rd Conjugation:
pectō, pectere, pexī, pexus — *to comb*
vēndō, vēndere, vēndidī, vēnditus — *to sell*

Irregular:
ineō, inīre, iniī or inīvī, initus — *to go into, enter*

WORDS AND PHRASES:
cuius — *whose*
in quibus — *among whom*
Quam ob causam...? — *For what reason...? Why...?*

Chapter 29

NOUNS:

1st Declension:

flamma, -ae, f.	*flame*
mēnsa, -ae, f.	***table***
rixa, -ae, f.	*quarrel*

2nd Declension:

fūmus, -ī, m.	***smoke***
lībertus, -ī, m.	***freedman***
mendīcus, -ī, m.	*beggar*

3rd Declension:

adstantēs, adstantium, m. pl.	*bystanders*
fīnis, fīnis, gen. pl., **fīnium,** m.	***end***
vestis, vestis, gen. pl., **vestium,** f.	***clothing, garment***

4th Declension:

versus, -ūs, m.	*verse, line (of poetry)*

ADJECTIVES:

1st and 2nd Declension:

celerrimus, -a, -um	***fastest, very fast***
ēlegantissimus, -a, -um	***most elegant***

Indefinite Adjective: **quīdam, quaedam, quoddam** *(a) certain*

Interrogative Adjective: **Quī...? Quae...? Quod...?** *What...? Which...?*

PRONOUN:

Interrogative Pronoun: **Quis...? Quid...?** *Who...? What...?*

PREPOSITION: **ā, ab** + abl. *from, by*

VERBS:

1st Conjugation:

concursō, -āre, -āvī, -ātūrus	*to run to and fro, run about*
dēlectō, -āre, -āvī, -ātus	***to delight, amuse***
recitō, -āre, -āvī, -ātus	*to read aloud, recite*

3rd Conjugation:

recumbō, recumbere, recubuī	***to recline, lie down***
rumpō, rumpere, rūpī, ruptus	***to burst***

3rd Conjugation (-iō):

aufugiō, aufugere, aufūgī	***to run away, escape***
ēripiō, ēripere, ēripuī, ēreptus	*to snatch (from)*

4th Conjugation:

grunniō, -īre	*to grunt*

WORDS AND PHRASES:

portātur	***is (being) carried***
recitāns	*reciting*
summā celeritāte	***with the greatest speed***

Chapter 30

NOUNS:

1st Declension:

fenestra, -ae, f.	*window*
incola, -ae, m./f.	*inhabitant, tenant*
īnsula, -ae, f.	*island, apartment building*

2nd Declension:

dubium, -ī, n.	*doubt*
incendium, -ī, n.	*fire*
ōrnāmenta, -ōrum, n. pl.	*furnishings*
spectāculum, -ī, n.	*sight, spectacle*
tabulātum, -ī, n.	*story, floor*

3rd Declension:

īnfāns, īnfantis, m./f.	*infant, young child*
pariēs, parietis, m.	*wall (of a house or room)*

Irregular:

vīs, acc., **vim**, abl., **vī**, f.	*force, amount*

ADJECTIVES:

1st and 2nd Declension:

īnfirmus, -a, -um	*weak, shaky, frail*
parvus, -a, -um	*small*

3rd Declension:

miserābilis, -is, -e	*miserable, wretched*

ADVERBS:

paene	*almost*
tam	*so*

CONJUNCTION:

ac	*and*

VERBS:

1st Conjugation:

obscūrō, -āre, -āvī, -ātus	*to hide*

2nd Conjugation:

commoveō, commovēre, commōvī, commōtus	*to move, upset*

3rd Conjugation:

ēmittō, ēmittere, ēmīsī, ēmissus	*to send out*
exstinguō, exstinguere, exstīnxī, exstīnctus	*to put out, extinguish*
opprimō, opprimere, oppressī, oppressus	*to overwhelm*
quaerō, quaerere, quaesīvī, quaesītus	*to seek, look for, ask (for)*

3rd Conjugation (-iō):

ēiciō, ēicere, ēiēcī, ēiectus	*to throw out*

Irregular

efferō, efferre, extulī, ēlātus	*to carry out, bring out*

Chapter 31

NOUNS:

1st Declension:

convīva, -ae, m.	*guest (at a banquet)*
perna, -ae, f.	*ham*
umbra, -ae, f.	*shadow, shade (of the dead)*

2nd Declension:

cachinnus, -ī, m.	*laughter*
dēnārius, -ī, m.	*denarius (silver coin)*
lanius, -ī, m.	*butcher*
pretium, -ī, n.	*price*
trīclīnium, -ī, n.	*dining room*

3rd Declension:

carō, carnis, f.	*meat*
lepus, leporis, m.	*hare*

ADJECTIVES:

1st and 2nd Declension:

fidēlissimus, -a, -um	*most faithful, very faithful*
multus, -a, -um	*much*
nōtus, -a, -um	*known*
optimus, -a, -um	*best, very good, excellent*

3rd Declension:

celeber, celebris, celebre	*famous*
pinguis, -is, -e	*fat*
procāx, procācis	*insolent*; as slang, *pushy*

DEMONSTRATIVE ADJECTIVES AND PRONOUNS:

īdem, eadem, idem	*the same*
ipse, ipsa, ipsum	*himself, herself, itself, themselves, very*

ADVERBS:

grātīs	*free, for nothing*
immō	*rather, on the contrary*
magnopere	*greatly*
quidem	*indeed*
rēctē	*rightly, properly*
umquam	*ever*
vērō	*truly, really, indeed*

CONJUNCTION:

autem	*however, but*

PREPOSITION:

ā, ab + abl.	*from, by*

VERBS:

2nd Conjugation: retineō, retinēre, retinuī, retentus   *to hold back, keep*

3rd Conjugation:

addō, addere, addidī, additus	*to add*
bibō, bibere, bibī	*to drink*
dēpōnō, dēpōnere, dēposuī, dēpositus	*to lay down, put aside, set down*
minuō, minuere, minuī, minūtus	*to lessen, reduce, decrease*
pāscō, pāscere, pāvī, pāstus	*to feed, pasture*
reprehendō, reprehendere, reprehendī, reprehēnsus	*to blame, scold, reprove*

3rd Conjugation (-iō):

accipiō, accipere, accēpī, acceptus	*to receive, get, welcome*

WORD: Quantī...?   *How much...?*

Chapter 32

NOUNS:

1st Declension: solea, -ae, f. *sandal*

2nd Declension: candēlābrum, -ī, n. *candelabrum, lamp-stand*

Cerberus, -ī, m. *Cerberus (three-headed dog guarding the underworld)*

iēntāculum, -ī, n *breakfast*

īnferī, -ōrum, m. pl. *the underworld*

iussa, -ōrum, n. pl. *commands, orders*

mālum, -ī, n. ***apple***

Mercurius, -ī, m. *Mercury (messenger god)*

oleum, -ī, n. *oil*

Orpheus, -ī, m. *Orpheus (legendary singer and husband of Eurydice)*

ōvum, -ī, n. ***egg***

pallium, -ī, n. *cloak*

prandium, -ī, n. *midday meal*

pullus, -ī, m. *chicken*

rēgnum, -ī, n. ***kingdom***

strātum, -ī, n. *sheet, covering*

3rd Declension: Charōn, Charōnis, m. *Charon (ferryman in the underworld)*

holus, holeris, n. *vegetable*

ignis, ignis, gen. pl., ignium, m. ***fire***

pānis, pānis, m. ***bread***

Plūtōn, Plūtōnis, m. *Pluto (king of the underworld)*

ADJECTIVES:

1st and 2nd Declension: ōrnātissimus, -a, -um *very decorated*

pulcherrimus, -a, -um ***most/very beautiful***

3rd Declension: **complūrēs, -ēs, -a** ***several, many***

ADVERB: **cōmiter** ***courteously, graciously, in a friendly way***

PREPOSITION: **circum** + acc. ***around***

VERBS:

1st Conjugation: **comparō, -āre, -āvī, -ātus** ***to buy, obtain, get ready***

3rd Conjugation:
accumbō, accumbere, accubuī, accubitūrus ***to recline (at table)***

addūcō, addūcere, addūxī, adductus *to lead on, bring*

coquō, coquere, coxī, coctus ***to cook***

effundō, effundere, effūdī, effūsus	*to pour out*; pass., *to be spilled, to spill*
ēvertō, ēvertere, ēvertī, ēversus	**to overturn, upset**

3rd Conjugation (-iō): **dēiciō, dēicere, dēiēcī, dēiectus** *to throw down*; pass., ***to fall***
reficiō, reficere, refēcī, refectus *to remake, redo, restore*

Irregular: **afferō, afferre, attulī, allātus** **to bring, bring to, bring in**
auferō, auferre, abstulī, ablātus **to carry away, take away**

WORDS AND PHRASES: Bonō animō es!/este! *Be of good mind! Cheer up!*
cāsū **by chance, accidentally**
quā dē causā *for this reason*

Chapter 33

NOUNS:

1st Declension:

anima, -ae, f.	*soul, "heart"*
lūna, -ae, f.	*moon*
olīva, -ae, f.	*olive*
pestilentia, -ae, f.	*plague*
popīna, -ae, f.	*eating-house, bar*
stēla, -ae, f.	*tombstone*
umbra, -ae, f.	*shadow, shade (of the dead)*
ūva, -ae, f.	*grape, bunch of grapes*

2nd Declension:

asparagus, -ī, m.	*asparagus*
bōlētus, -ī, m.	*mushroom*
coquus, -ī, m.	*cook*
ferculum, -ī, n.	*dish, tray*
frustum, -ī, n.	*scrap*
locus, -ī, m.	*place*
medicus, -ī, m.	*doctor*
mulsum, -ī, n.	*wine sweetened with honey*
nāsus, -ī, m.	*nose*
passum, -ī, n.	*raisin-wine*
pirum, -ī, n.	*pear*
pōculum, -ī, n.	*cup, goblet*
vestīmentum, -ī, n.	*clothing;* pl., *clothes*

3rd Declension:

gustātiō, gustātiōnis, f.	*hors d'oeuvre, first course*
liquāmen, liquāminis, n.	*garum (a sauce made from fish, used to season food)*
pecus, pecoris, n.	*livestock, sheep and cattle*
sanguis, sanguinis, m.	*blood*
versipellis, versipellis, gen. pl, versipellium, m.	*werewolf*

ADJECTIVES:

1st and 2nd Declension:

aspersus, -a, -um	*sprinkled*
cēterī, -ae, -a	*the rest (of), the other(s)*
īrātissimus, -a, -um	*most/very angry*
lapideus, -a, -um	*of stone, stony*
niger, nigra, nigrum	*black*
proximus, -a, -um	*nearest*
situs, -a, -um	*located, situated*
urbānus, -a, -um	*of the city/town*

ADVERBS:

forte	*by chance*
merīdiē	*at noon*
posteā	*afterward*
prius	*earlier*
ūnā	*together*

CONJUNCTIONS:	dōnec	*until*
	tamquam	*just as if*

PREPOSITION:	inter + acc.	*between, among*

INTERJECTION:	Euge!	*Hurray!*

VERBS:

1st Conjugation:

dēdicō, -āre, -āvī, -ātus	*to dedicate*
excūsō, -āre, -āvī, -ātus	*to forgive, excuse*
gustō, -āre, -āvī, -ātus	*to take a bite of*
numerō, -āre, -āvī, -ātus	*to count*
ululō, -āre, -āvī, -ātus	*to howl*
vulnerō, -āre, -āvī, -ātus	*to wound*

2nd Conjugation:

careō, carēre, caruī, caritūrus + abl.	*to need, lack*
compleō, complēre, complēvī, complētus	*to fill*
dērīdeō, dērīdēre, dērīsī, dērīsus	*to laugh at, get the last laugh*

3rd Conjugation:

caedō, caedere, cecīdī, caesus	*to strike, cut down, kill*
exuō, exuere, exuī, exūtus	*to take off*
irrumpō, irrumpere, irrūpī, irruptus	*to burst in*
prōcēdō, prōcēdere, prōcessī, prōcessūrus	*to go forward*
scindō, scindere, scidī, scissus	*to cut, split, carve*

Irregular:

edō, ēsse, ēdī, ēsus	*to eat*

WORDS AND PHRASES:

dē porcō datum est	*some pork was given*
Dī immortālēs	*Immortal gods! Good heavens!*
rēs urbānae, rērum urbānārum, f. pl.	*affairs of the city/town*
sē excusāre	*to apologize*
secundae mēnsae, -ārum, f. pl.	*second course, dessert*

Chapter 34

NOUNS:

1st Declension:

arānea, -ae, f.	*cobweb*
corōna, -ae, f.	*garland, crown*
cūra, -ae, f.	***care***
hedera, -ae, f.	*ivy*
rosa, -ae, f.	*rose*

2nd Declension:

apium, -ī, n.	*parsley*
convīvium, -ī, n.	***feast, banquet***
cyathus, -ī, m.	*small ladle, measure (of wine)*
fritillus, -ī, m.	*cylindrical box*
merum, -ī, n.	*undiluted wine*
modus, -ī, m.	***way, method***
sacculus, -ī, m.	*small bag (used for holding money)*
tālī, -ōrum, m. pl.	*knucklebones*
unguentum, -ī, n.	*ointment, perfume*

3rd Declension:

amor, amōris, m.	*love*
canis, canis, m./f.	***dog; the lowest throw of the knucklebones***
cōmissātiō, cōmissātiōnis, f.	*drinking party*
Cupīdō, Cupīdinis, m.	*Cupid (the son of Venus)*
flōs, flōris, m.	*flower*
Herculēs, Herculis, m.	*Hercules (Greek hero)*
sal, salis, m.	***salt, wit***
sēniō, sēniōnis, m.	*the six (in throwing knucklebones)*
Venus, Veneris, f.	*Venus (the goddess of love); the highest throw of the knucklebones*

Indeclinable:

nīl	***nothing***

ADJECTIVES:

1st and 2nd Declension:

candidus, -a, -um	*white, fair-skinned, beautiful*
ēbrius, -a, -um	***drunk***
foedus, -a, -um	***filthy, disgusting***
merus, -a, -um	*pure*
paucī, -ae, -a	***few***
pessimus, -a, -um	***worst***
venustus, -a, -um	*charming*

3rd Declension:

abstinēns, abstinentis + abl.	*refraining from*
ācer, ācris, ācre	***keen, bitter, sharp***
brevis, -is, -e	***short***
celer, celeris, celere	***fast, swift***
difficilis, -is, -e	***difficult***
dissimilis, -is, -e	***unlike, dissimilar***
facilis, -is, -e	***easy***

fēlīx, fēlīcis	*lucky, happy, fortunate*
gracilis, -is, -e	*slender*
humilis, -is, -e	*humble*
prūdēns, prūdentis	*wise, sensible*
similis, -is, -e + gen. or dat.	*similar (to), like*
suāvis, -is, -e	*sweet, delightful*
vetus, veteris	*old*

ADVERBS:

contrā	*in return*
magis	*more*
maximē	*most, very much*
nimis*	*too much*
optimē	*very well, excellently*
paulātim	*gradually*
prūdenter	*wisely, sensibly*
quam	*than*

*Adverb or indeclinable substantive

CONJUNCTIONS:

et...et	*both...and*
seu = sive	*or if*
-ve, enclitic	*or*

VERBS:

1st Conjugation:

corōnō, -āre, -āvī, -ātus	*to crown*
creō, -āre, -āvī, -ātus	*to appoint*
dōnō, -āre, -āvī, -ātus	*to give*
invocō, -āre, -āvī, -ātus	*to invoke, call upon*

2nd Conjugation:

misceō, miscēre, miscuī, mixtus	*to mix*
placeō, -ēre, -uī + dat.	*to please*

3rd Conjugation:

poscō, poscere, poposcī	*to demand, ask for*
sinō, sinere, sīvī, situs	*to allow*

4th Conjugation:

hauriō, haurīre, hausī, haustus	*to drain*

Irregular:

fīō, fierī, factus sum	*to become, be made, be done, happen*

WORDS AND PHRASES:

arbiter bibendī	*master of the drinking*
collāpsus est	*he collapsed*
in diēs	*every day, day by day*
inquam	*I say*
nē...quidem	*not even*
plūs vīnī	*more wine*
quam celerrimē	*as quickly as possible*

Chapter 35

NOUNS:

1st Declension:

Subūra, -ae, f.	*Subura (a district of Rome off the Forum, known for its night life)*

2nd Declension:

deus, -ī, m.	*god*
tergum, -ī, n.	*back, rear*

3rd Declension:

collis, collis, gen. pl., **collium,** m.	*hill*
difficultās, difficultātis, f.	*difficulty*
fūstis, fūstis, gen. pl., fūstium, m.	*club, cudgel*
timor, timōris, m.	*fear*
vulnus, vulneris, n.	*wound*

ADJECTIVES:

1st and 2nd Declension:

affectus, -a, -um	*affected, overcome*
certus, -a, -um	*certain*
lentus, -a, -um	*slow*
prōnus, -a, -um	*face down*
rēctus, -a, -um	*right, proper*
sēcūrus, -a, -um	*carefree, unconcerned*
summus, -a, -um	*greatest, very great*

3rd Declension:

dīligēns, dīligentis	*diligent, painstaking, thorough*
ferōx, ferōcis	*fierce*
gravis, -is, -e	*heavy, serious*
Quirīnālis, -is, -e	*Quirinal (referring to the Quirinal Hill, one of the seven hills of Rome)*
vehemēns, vehementis	*violent*

ADVERBS:

breviter	*briefly*
fortissimē	*most/very bravely*
longē	*far*

VERBS:

1st Conjugation:

ligō, -āre, -āvī, -ātus	*to bind up*

3rd Conjugation:

adimō, adimere, adēmī, adēmptus + dat.	*to take away (from)*
concurrō, concurrere, concurrī, concursūrus	*to run together, rush up*
crēdō, crēdere, crēdidī, crēditus + dat.	*to trust, believe*
dēfendō, dēfendere, dēfendī, dēfēnsus	*to defend*

3rd Conjugation (iō):

corripiō, corripere, corripuī, correptus	*to seize, grab*
percutiō, percutere, percussī, percussus	*to strike*

PHRASE:

cōnsecūtī sunt	*they overtook*

Chapter 36

NOUNS:

1st Declension:

Bīthȳnia, -ae, f.	*Bithynia (province in Asia Minor)*
Kalendae, -ārum, f. pl.	*the Kalends (1st day of the month)*
Nōnae, -ārum, f. pl.	*the Nones*

2nd Declension:

Brundisium, -ī, n.	*Brundisium*
Brundisiī	*in/at Brundisium*
Brundisium	*to Brundisium*
Brundisiō	*from Brundisium*

3rd Declension:

adulēscēns, adulēscentis, m.	***young man, youth***
cōnsul, cōnsulis, m.	***consul***

4th Declension:

Īdūs, Īduum, f. pl.	*the Ides*

ADJECTIVES:

3rd Declension:

audāx, audācis	***bold***
trīstis, -is, -e	***sad***

Months:

Iānuārius, -a, -um	*of January*
Februārius, -a, -um	*of February*
Mārtius, -a, -um	*of March*
Aprīlis, -is, -e	*of April*
Maius, -a, -um	*of May*
Iūnius, -a, -um	*of June*
Iūlius, -a -um	*of July*
Augustus, -a, -um	*of August*
September, Septembris, Septembre	*of September*
Octōber, Octōbris, Octōbre	*of October*
November, Novembris, Novembre	*of November*
December, Decembris, Decembre	*of December*

Indeclinable:

vīgintī	*twenty*

ADVERBS:

hūc	***here, to here***
libenter	***gladly***
prīdiē + acc.	*on the day before*
rūrsus	***again***
sānē	***certainly, of course***

CONJUNCTION:

-que, enclitic	***and***

PREPOSITION:

ante + acc.	*before*

VERBS:

2nd Conjugation:

persuādeō, persuādēre, persuāsī, persuāsus

to make something (acc.)
agreeable to someone (dat.), *to persuade someone of something*

3rd Conjugation: condō, condere, condidī, conditus

to found

WORDS AND PHRASES:

a.d. iii Kal. Dec. = ante diem tertium Kalendās Decembrēs	*on November 29*
cōnātus est	***(he) tried***
Īdibus Novembribus	*on November 13*
Kalendīs Novembribus	*on November 1*
morātus est	***he has stayed***
Nōnīs Novembribus	*on November 5*
prīdiē Īdūs Octōbrēs	*on October 14*
proficīscētur	***(he/she) will set out***
quī hominēs	*which/those men*
quō celerius...eō celerius	***the faster... the faster...***
regressus est	***he has returned***
S. D. (salūtem dīcit)	*(he/she) sends greetings*
S. P. D. (salūtem plūrimam dīcit)	*(he/she) sends fondest greetings*
secūtī sunt	***(they) followed***
sīs = sī vīs	*if you wish, please*

Chapter 37

NOUNS:

1st Declension:

lanterna, -ae, f.	*lantern*
scriblīta, -ae, f.	*tart or pastry with cheese filling*

2nd Declension:

grammaticus, -ī, m.	***secondary school teacher***
iēntāculum, -ī, n.	*breakfast*
lūdus, -ī, m.	***school***
magister, magistrī, m.	***schoolmaster***
paedagōgus, -ī, m.	***tutor***
paulum, -ī, n.	***a small amount, a little***
pīstrīnum, -ī, n.	*bakery*
Vergilius, -ī, m.	*Vergil (Roman poet)*

ADJECTIVES:

1st and 2nd Declension:

ērudītus, -a, -um	***learned, scholarly***
sextus, -a, -um	***sixth***

3rd Declension:

ūtilis, -is, -e	***useful***

ADVERB:

cotīdiē	***daily, every day***

CONJUNCTIONS:

etiamsī	*even if*
vel	*or*

VERBS:

1st Conjugation:

castīgō, -āre, -āvī, -ātus	***to rebuke, reprimand***

2nd Conjugation:

vereor, verērī, veritus sum	***to be afraid, fear***

3rd Conjugation:

colloquor, colloquī, collocūtus sum	*to converse, speak together*
loquor, loquī, locūtus sum	*to speak, talk*

3rd Conjugation (-iō):

ēgredior, ēgredī, ēgressus sum	***to go out, leave***
ingredior, ingredī, ingressus sum	***to go in, enter***

4th Conjugation:

experior, experīrī, expertus sum	***to test, try***

Irregular:

praeferō, praeferre, praetulī, praelātus	*to carry X* (acc.) *in front of Y* (dat.)

WORDS AND PHRASES:

ad tempus	*on time*
memoriā tenēre	*to remember*

Chapter 38

NOUNS:

1st Declension:

Aenēās, Aenēae, m.	*Aeneas (son of Venus and Anchises and legendary ancestor of the Romans)*
Āfrica, -ae, f.	*Africa*
Hesperia, -ae, f.	*Hesperia (the land in the West, Italy)*
rēgīna, -ae, f.	***queen***
ruīna, -ae, f.	***collapse, ruin***
Sicilia, -ae, f.	*Sicily*
terra, -ae, f.	***earth, ground, land***
Troia, -ae, f.	*Troy*

2nd Declension:

annus, -ī, m.	***year***
discipulus, -ī, m.	***pupil***
respōnsum, -ī, n.	*reply*
torus, -ī, m.	*couch*

3rd Declension:

Aenēis, Aenēidis, f.	*the Aeneid (an epic poem by Vergil)*
Dīdō, Dīdōnis, f.	*Dido (queen of Carthage)*
dolor, dolōris, m.	*grief*
mare, maris, abl. sing., **marī,** gen. pl., **marium,** n.	***sea***
mēnsis, mēnsis, m.	***month***
nāvis, nāvis, gen. pl., **nāvium,** f.	***ship***
ōs, ōris, n.	*mouth, face*
tempestās, tempestātis, f.	***storm***
Ulixēs, Ulixis, m.	*Ulysses, Odysseus (Greek hero of the Trojan War)*

ADJECTIVES:

1st and 2nd Declension:

aliquī, -ae, -a	***some***
altus, -a, -um	*tall, high, lofty, deep*
īnfandus, -a, -um	*unspeakable*
intentus, -a, -um	*intent, eager*
Troiānus, -a, -um	*Trojan*

ADVERB:

inde	*from there, then*

INTERROGATIVE WORDS:

Quot...?	***How many...?***
Quotus, -a, -um....?	***Which (in numerical order)...?***

VERBS:

1st Conjugation:	**nāvigō, -āre, -āvī, -ātus**	*to sail*
	renovō, -āre, -āvī, -ātus	*to renew, revive*
2nd Conjugation:	**dēleō, dēlēre, dēlēvī, dēlētus**	*to destroy*
	obsideō, obsidēre, obsēdī, obsessus	*to besiege*
3rd Conjugation:	conticēscō, conticēscere, conticuī	*to become silent*
	incendō, incendere, incendī, incēnsus	*to burn, set on fire*
3rd Conjugation (-iō):	**patior, patī, passus sum**	*to suffer, endure*
4th Conjugation:	ōrdior, ōrdīrī, ōrsus sum	*to begin*

WORD:

	coepit	*(he/she/it) began*

Chapter 39

NOUNS:

1st Declension:

Athēnae, -ārum, f. pl.	*Athens*
Baiae, -ārum, f. pl.	*Baiae*
Cremōna, -ae, f.	*Cremona (town in northern Italy)*
Crēta, -ae, f.	*Crete (large island southeast of Greece)*
ferula, -ae, f.	*cane*
Gallia, -ae, f.	*Gaul*
Hispania, -ae, f.	*Spain*
lingua, -ae, f.	***tongue, language***
litterae, -ārum, f. pl.	***letters, literature***
Mantua, -ae, f.	*Mantua (town in northern Italy)*
ōra, -ae, f.	***shore***
Thrācia, -ae, f.	*Thrace (country northeast of Greece)*

2nd Declension:

altum, -ī, n.	***the deep, the sea***
arma, -ōrum, n. pl.	***arms, weapons***
Augustus, -ī, m.	*Augustus (first Roman emperor)*
bellum, -ī, n.	***war***
Dēlōs, -ī, f.	*Delos (small island off the eastern coast of Greece)*
deus, -ī, nom. pl., **dī,** dat., abl. pl., **dīs,** m.	***god***
fātum, -ī, n.	***fate***
fundus, -ī, m.	*farm*
Horātius, -ī, m.	*Horace (Roman poet)*
Latium, -ī, n.	*Latium (the area of central Italy that included Rome)*
Mediolānum, -ī, n.	*Milan*
oppidum, -ī, n.	***town***
Philippī, -ōrum, m. pl.	*Philippi*
superī, -ōrum, m. pl	***the gods above***
verbum, -ī, n.	***word, verb***

3rd Declension:

Alpēs, Alpium, f. pl.	*the Alps*
Carthāgō, Carthāginis, f.	*Carthage (city on the northern coast of Africa)*
comes, comitis, m./f.	***companion***
genus, generis, n.	***race, stock, nation***
hiems, hiemis, f.	***winter***
Iūnō, Iūnōnis, f.	*Juno (queen of the gods)*
lītus, lītoris, n.	***shore***
moenia, moenium, n. pl.	***city walls***
procācitās, procācitātis, f.	*insolence*
rūs, rūris, n.	***country, country estate***
Sīdōn, Sīdōnis, f.	*Sidon*
sōlitūdō, sōlitūdinis, f.	*solitude*
valētūdō, valētūdinis, f.	*health (good or bad)*

4th Declension:

domus, -ūs, f.	***house, home***

ADJECTIVES:

1st and 2nd Declension:

abōminandus, -a, -um	*detestable, horrible*
aeger, aegra, aegrum	***ill***
Albānus, -a, -um	*of Alba Longa (city founded by Aeneas's son, Ascanius)*
Latīnus, -a, -um	*Latin*
Lāvīnius, -a, -um	*of Lavinium (name of the town first settled by the Trojans in Italy)*
profugus, -a, -um	*exiled, fugitive*
saevus, -a, -um	***fierce, savage***
territus, -a, -um	*frightened*

3rd Declension:

memor, memoris	***remembering, mindful, unforgetting***
septentriōnālis, -is, -e	*northern*
terribilis, -is, -e	*frightening*
virīlis, -is, -e	***of manhood***

ADVERBS:

abhinc	***back from this point in time, ago, previously***
ante	***previously, before***
interdum	*from time to time*
nusquam	***nowhere***
post	***after(ward), later***
sīc	***thus, in this way***

CONJUNCTION:

antequam	*before*

PREPOSITIONS:

ante + acc.	***before, in front of***
ob + acc.	***on account of***
post + acc.	***after***
trāns + acc.	***across***

VERBS:

1st Conjugation:

aegrōtō, -āre, -āvī, -ātūrus	*to be ill*
dormitō, -āre, -āvī	*to be sleepy*
iactō, -āre, -āvī, -ātus	***to toss about, drive to and fro***
migrō, -āre, -āvī, -ātūrus	*to move one's home*

2nd Conjugation:

moneō, -ēre, -uī, -itus	***to advise, warn***
pāreō, -ēre, -uī, -itūrus + dat.	***to obey***
studeō, -ēre, -uī + dat.	***to study***

3rd Conjugation:

animadvertō, animadvertere, animadvertī, animadversus	***to notice***
canō, canere, cecinī, cantus	***to sing***
expellō, expellere, expulī, expulsus	***to drive out, expel***
expergīscor, expergīscī, experrēctus sum	*to wake up*

extendō, extendere, extendī, extentus	*to hold out*
nāscor, nāscī, nātus sum	*to be born*
omittō, omittere, omīsī, omissus	*to leave out, omit*
vīvō, vīvere, vīxī, vīctūrus	*to live*

3rd Conjugation (-iō):   **morior, morī, mortuus sum**   *to die*

4th Conjugation: **sepeliō, sepelīre, sepelīvī, sepultus**   *to bury*

Irregular: īnferō, īnferre, intulī, illātus   *to bring in*

WORDS AND PHRASES:

fīnem recitandī fēcit	*(he) made an end of reciting, (he) stopped reciting*
idem ac	*the same as*
īnfirmā...valētūdine	*in poor health*
interest	***it is important***
in terram ēgressus	*having disembarked*
multīs post annīs	*many years afterward*
recitandī	*of reciting*
rediēns	*returning*
toga virīlis, togae virīlis, f.	*toga of manhood, plain white toga*

Chapter 40

NOUNS:

1st Declension:

īrācundia, -ae, f.	*irritability, bad temper*
poena, -ae, f.	**punishment, penalty**
scapha, -ae, f.	*small boat*

2nd Declension:

Pompeiī, -ōrum, m. pl.	*Pompeii*
templum, -ī, n.	*temple*

3rd Declension:

rogātiō, rogātiōnis, f.	*question*

ADJECTIVES:

1st and 2nd Declension:

īrācundus, -a, -um	*irritable, in a bad mood*
vērus, -a, -um	*true*

3rd Declension:

crūdēlis, -is, -e	*cruel*

ADVERBS:

immō vērō	**on the contrary, in fact**
inde	*from there, then*
prīmō	*first, at first*
quam prīmum	*as soon as possible*

CONJUNCTIONS:

cum	*when, since*
cum prīmum	*as soon as*

VERBS:

1st Conjugation:

ignōrō, -āre, -āvī, -ātus	*to be ignorant, not to know*
natō, -āre, -āvī, -ātūrus	*to swim*
obsecrō, -āre, -āvī, -ātus	*to beseech, beg*

2nd Conjugation:

audeō, audēre, ausus sum + inf.	*to dare (to)*
gaudeō, gaudēre, gāvīsus sum	*to be glad, rejoice*
soleō, solēre, solitus sum + inf.	*to be accustomed (to), be in the habit of*
valeō, -ēre, -uī, -itūrus	*to be strong, be well*

3rd Conjugation:

arcessō, arcessere, arcessīvī, arcessītus	*to summon, send for*
discō, discere, didicī	*to learn*
repellō, repellere, reppulī, repulsus	*to drive off, drive back*

3rd Conjugation (-iō):

cupiō, cupere, cupīvī, cupītus	*to desire, want*
rapiō, rapere, rapuī, raptus	*to snatch, seize*

4th Conjugation:

dēsiliō, dēsilīre, dēsiluī	*to leap down*

WORDS AND PHRASES:

Avē! Avēte!	*Greetings!*
poenās dare	**to pay the penalty, be punished**
Pompeiīs	*in Pompeii*
vēra dīcere	**to tell the truth**

Chapter 41

NOUNS:
1st Declension: tēla, -ae, f. *web, fabric*

2nd Declension: **studium, -ī, n.** ***enthusiasm, study***

3rd Declension: **tālia, -ium, n. pl.** *such things*

ADVERBS: forās *outside*

Quantum...! *How much...!*

VERB:
3rd Conjugation: ēripiō, ēripere, ēripuī, ēreptus *to snatch from, rescue*

texō, texere, texuī, textus *to weave*

WORDS AND PHRASES: dīcitur *(he/she/it) is said*

discessisse *to have departed*

Chapter 42

NOUNS:

1st Declension:

casa, -ae, f.	*hut, cottage*
unda, -ae, f.	*wave*

2nd Declension:

magister, magistrī, m.	*schoolmaster, master, captain*
ventus, -ī, m.	*wind*

3rd Declension:

pūgiō, pūgiōnis, m.	*dagger*

ADJECTIVES:

1st and 2nd Declension:

armātus, -a, -um	*armed*

3rd Declension:

dīves, dīvitis	*rich*
pauper, pauperis	*poor*

ADVERB:

clam	*secretly*

CONJUNCTION:

quoniam	*since*

VERBS:

1st Conjugation:

superō, -āre, -āvī, -ātus	*to overcome*

3rd Conjugation:

convalēscō, convalēscere, convaluī	*to grow stronger, get well*
ēvādō, ēvādere, ēvāsī, ēvāsus	*to escape*
redūcō, redūcere, redūxī, reductus	*to lead back, take back*
resistō, resistere, restitī + dat.	*to resist*

4th Conjugation:

adorior, adorīrī, adortus sum	*to attack*
coorior, coorīrī, coortus sum	*to rise up, arise*

PHRASE:

Prō dī immortālēs!	*Good heavens!*

Chapter 43

NOUNS:

1st Declension:

balneae, -ārum, f. p.	*baths*
palaestra, -ae, f.	*exercise ground*
thermae, -ārum, f. pl.,	*public baths*

2nd Declension:

apodytērium, -ī, n.	*changing room (at the baths)*
caldārium, -ī, n.	*hot room (at the baths)*
digitus, -ī, m.	***finger***
frīgidārium, -ī, n.	*cold room (at the baths)*
harpastum, -ī, n.	*heavy handball*
linteum, -ī, n.	*towel*
pālus, -ī, m.	*post*
tepidārium, -ī, n.	*warm room (at the baths)*
unguentum, -ī, n.	*ointment, perfume, oil*
vestibulum, -ī, n.	***entrance passage***

3rd Declension:

calor, calōris, m.	***heat***
follis, follis, gen. pl., follium, m.	*bag*
senex, senis, m.	***old man***
strigilis, strigilis, gen. pl., strigilium, f.	*strigil, scraper*
trigōn, trigōnis, m.	*ball game involving three people, ball (used in this game)*
vapor, vapōris, m.	*steam*

ADJECTIVES:

1st and 2nd Declension:

calvus, -a, -um	*bald*
capillātus, -a, -um	*with long hair*
indūtus, -a, -um	***clothed***
Nerōnēus, -a, -um	*of Nero*
rīdiculus, -a, -um	*absurd, laughable*
varius, -a, -um	*different, various, varied, many-hued*

ADVERBS:

haud	***not***
quō	***there, to that place***

PREPOSITION:

contrā + acc.	***against***

VERBS:

1st Conjugation:

concrepō, concrepāre, concrepuī	*to snap (the fingers)*
dēfricō, dēfricāre, dēfricuī, dēfrictus	*to rub down*
lūctor, -ārī, -ātus sum	*to wrestle*

2nd Conjugation:

exerceō, -ēre, -uī, -itus	***to exercise, train***
tergeō, tergēre, tersī, tersus	*to dry, wipe*

3rd Conjugation:

cognōscō, cognōscere, cognōvī, cognitus	*to find out, learn*
repetō, repetere, repetīvī, repetītus	*to pick up, recover*
unguō, unguere, ūnxī, ūnctus	*to anoint, smear with oil*

4th Conjugation:

conveniō, convenīre, convēnī, conventūrus	*to come together, meet, assemble*

WORDS AND PHRASES:

Campus Mārtius, -ī, m.	*the Plain of Mars on the outskirts of Rome*
pecūniā datā	*his money having been given, after paying his entrance fee*
Thermae Nerōnēae, -ārum, f. pl.	*the Baths of Nero*
vīnō sūmptō	*wine having been taken, after a drink of wine*

Chapter 44

NOUNS:

1st Declension: sella, -ae, f. *sedan chair, seat, chair*

2nd Declension: pavīmentum, -ī, n. *tiled floor*

3rd Declension: fūr, fūris, m. *thief*

VERBS:

3rd Conjugation: lābor, lābī, lāpsus sum *to slip, fall*
prehendō, prehendere, prehendī, prehēnsus *to seize*
subsequor, subsequī, subsecūtus sum *to follow (up)*

3rd Conjugation(-iō): cōnfugiō, cōnfugere, cōnfūgī *to flee for refuge*
surripiō, surripere, surripuī, surreptus *to steal*

4th Conjugation: exsiliō, exsilīre, exsiluī *to leap out*

WORDS AND PHRASES:

exeāmus *let us go out*
mē custōde *me on guard, while I am on guard*
quibus verbīs audītīs *which words having been heard,*
when they had heard this

Chapter 45

NOUNS:

1st Declension:

lacrima, -ae, f.	*tear*
rīma, -ae, f.	*crack*
spēlunca, -ae, f.	*cave*
Thisbē, Thisbēs, f.	*Thisbe*

2nd Declension:

cōnsilium, -ī, n.	***plan***
ōsculum, -ī, n.	***kiss***
Pȳramus, -ī, m.	*Pyramus*

3rd Declension:

Babylōn, Babylōnis, f.	*Babylon*
leō, leōnis, m.	*lion*
recitātiō, recitātiōnis, f.	*recitation*
vēlāmen, vēlāminis, n.	*veil, shawl*
virgō, virginis, f.	***maiden***

4th Declension:

vultus, -ūs, m.	***face***

ADJECTIVES:

1st and 2nd Declension:

īnscius, -a, -um	***not knowing***
sanguineus, -a, -um	*bloodstained*
uterque, utraque, utrumque	***each (of two), both***

3rd Declension:

commūnis, -is, -e	*common*
prior, prior, prius, gen., priōris	***first (of two), previous***

ADVERBS:

noctū	*at/by night*
prope	*near, nearby, nearly*
sēcrētō	*secretly*

CONJUNCTION:

nec	***and...not***

VERBS:

1st Conjugation:

rixor, -ārī, -ātus sum	*to quarrel*

2nd Conjugation:

polliceor, pollicērī, pollicitus sum	***to promise***

3rd Conjugation:

aspergō, aspergere, aspersī, aspersus	*to sprinkle, splash, spatter*
exprimō, exprimere, expressī, expressus	***to press out, express***
occīdō, occīdere, occīdī, occīsus	***to kill***
perdō, perdere, perdidī, perditus	***to destroy***
valedīcō, valedīcere, valedīxī, valedictūrus	*to say goodbye*

3rd Conjugation (-iō):
          prōgredior, prōgredī, prōgressus sum   *to go forward, advance*

4th Conjugation: **orior, orīrī, ortus sum**   *to rise*
                          sentiō, sentīre, sēnsī, sēnsus   *to feel, notice*

WORDS AND PHRASES:

              cōnsilium capere   *to adopt a plan*
              moritūrus, -a, -um   *about to die, intending to*
                                    die, determined to die

              ōre sanguine aspersō   *his mouth spattered with blood*

Chapter 46

NOUNS:

1st Declension: pūpa, -ae, f.   *doll*

2nd Declension: **dōnum, -ī, n.**   ***gift***
                                  latrunculus, -ī, m.   *bandit, piece in a game like chess*
                                  lūdus, -ī, m.   *school, game*
                                  peristȳlium, -ī, n.   *peristyle (courtyard surrounded with a colonnade)*

5th Declension: merīdiēs, -ēī, m.   *noon, midday*

ADJECTIVE:

3rd Declension: nātālis, -is, -e   *of/belonging to birth*

ADVERBS: **ferē**   ***almost, approximately***
                                    postrēmō   ***finally***

VERBS:

1st Conjugation: micō, micāre, micuī   *to move quickly to and fro, flash*
                                  putō, -āre, -āvī, -ātus   ***to think, consider***

3rd Conjugation: ēdūcō, ēdūcere, ēdūxī, ēductus   *to lead out*
                                  laedō, laedere, laesī, laesus   ***to harm***

3rd Conjugation(-iō):   **abripiō, abripere, abripuī, abreptus**   ***to snatch away***

Irregular: **fīō, fierī, factus sum**   ***to become, be made, be done, happen***
                                  referō, referre, rettulī, relātus   *to bring back, report, write down*

WORDS AND PHRASES: **ambō, ambae, ambō**   ***both***
                                  capita aut nāvia   *heads or ship (a children's game)*
                                  diēs nātālis, diēī nātālis, m.   *birthday*
                                  digitīs micāre   *to play morra*
                                  dōnō (dat.) dare   *to give as a gift*
                                  lūdus latrunculōrum   *game of bandits (a game like chess)*
                                  Num...?   ***Surely...not...? (introduces a question that expects the answer "no"***
                                  pār impār   *odds or evens (a game)*
                                  Quid Sextō fīet?   *What will happen to Sextus?*

Chapter 47

NOUNS:

2nd Declension:	populus, -ī, m.	*people*
3rd Declension:	epigramma, epigrammatis, n.	*epigram*
	gladiātor, gladiātōris, m.	*gladiator*
	imperātor, imperātōris, m.	***commander, emperor***
	mūnera, mūnerum, n. pl.	***games***

ADJECTIVES:

1st and 2nd Declension:	**negōtiōsus, -a, -um**	***busy***
3rd Declension:	memorābilis, -is, -e	*memorable*

ADVERB:

mātūrē	*early*

VERBS:

1st Conjugation:	**spērō, -āre, -āvī, -ātus**	***to hope***
2nd Conjugation:	**contineō, continēre, continuī, contentus**	***to confine, hold***
3rd Conjugation (-iō):	congredior, congredī, congressus sum	*to come together, assemble*
Irregular:	**mālō, mālle, māluī**	***to prefer***

WORDS AND PHRASES:

cōnstat	***it is agreed***
epistula est cōnficienda	*the letter must be finished*
Mārtiālis, Mārcus Valerius, m.	*Martial (poet, ca. A.D. 40–104)*
māvult	***(he/she) prefers***
prō certō habēre	*to be sure*
quō maior..., eō plūs...	***the greater..., the more...***

Chapter 48

NOUNS:

1st Declension:

arēna, -ae, f.	*sand, arena*
dēliciae, -ārum, f. pl.	*delight*
dīvitiae, -ārum, f. pl.	*wealth, riches*
hasta, -ae, f.	*spear*
lanista, -ae, m.	*trainer*
lūdia, -ae, f.	*female slave attached to a gladiatorial school*
pugna, -ae, f.	*fight, battle*
tessera, -ae, f.	*ticket*
turba, -ae, f.	*crowd; cause of confusion/ turmoil*

2nd Declension:

locārius, -ī, m.	*scalper (a person who buys up seats and sells them for as high a price as he can get)*
magister, magistrī, m.	*school master, master, captain, trainer*
merīdiānī, -ōrum, m. pl.	*midday fighters*
saeculum, -ī, n.	*age, era*
suppositīcius, -ī, m.	*substitute*

3rd Declension:

admīrātio, admīrātiōnis, f.	*amazement*
aequor, aequoris, n.	*sea*
appāritor, appāritōris, m.	*public servant*
cassis, cassidis, f.	*plumed metal helmet*
cornicen, cornicinis, m.	*horn-player*
furor, furōris, m.	*frenzy*
mīlia, mīlium, n. pl.	*thousands*
paria, parium, n. pl.	*pairs*
pulvīnar, pulvīnāris, n.	*imperial seat (at the games)*
tremor, tremōris, m.	*cause of fright, terror*
tridēns, tridentis, gen. pl., tridentium, m.	*trident*
tubicen, tubicinis, m.	*trumpet-player*
voluptās, voluptātis, f.	*pleasure, delight*

ADJECTIVES:

1st and 2nd Declension:

aequoreus, -a, -um	*of/belonging to the sea*
belliger, belligera, belligerum	*warlike*
hūmānus, -a, -um	*human*
languidus, -a, -um	*drooping*
Mārtius, -a, -um	*connected with Mars (the god of war and combat)*
obstupefactus, -a, -um	*astounded*
superbus, -a, -um	*proud, arrogant*
timendus, -a, -um	*to be feared*
ūniversus, -a, -um	*the whole of, the entire*

3rd Declension:	mināx, minācis	*menacing*
Indeclinable:	tot	*so many*

ADVERBS:

	ācriter	*fiercely*
	aliās	*at another time*
	ter	*three times*

PREPOSITION:

	contrā + acc.	*against, opposite, in front of, facing*

VERBS:

1st Conjugation:

iugulō, -āre, -āvī, -ātus	*to kill, murder*
reservō, -āre, -āvī, -ātus	*to reserve*

3rd Conjugation:

committō, committere, commīsī, commissus	*to bring together*
cōnsistō, cōnsistere, cōnstitī	*to halt, stop, stand*
convertō, convertere, convertī, conversus	*to turn (around)*
incēdō, incēdere, incessī	*to go in, march in*
ostendō, ostendere, ostendī, ostentus	*to show, point out*

3rd Conjugation (-iō):

circumspiciō, circumspicere, circumspexī, circumspectus	*to look around*
coniciō, conicere, coniēcī, coniectus	*to throw, throw together; to figure out, guess*

4th Conjugation:

feriō, -īre	*to hit, strike, kill*

Irregular:

tollō, tollere, sustulī, sublātus	*to lift, raise*

WORDS AND PHRASES:

clāmātum est	*there was shouting*
crēdidissem	*I would have believed*
nōbīs redeundum est	*we must return*
pugnābātur	*the fighting went on*
pugnam committere	*to join battle*

Chapter 49

NOUNS:

1st Declension:

bēstia, -ae, f.	*beast*
cavea, -ae, f.	*cage*

2nd Declension:

bēstiārius, -ī, m.	*a person who fights wild beasts in the arena*

3rd Declension:

Androclēs, Androclis, m.	*Androcles*
crūdēlitās, crūdēlitātis, f.	***cruelty***
recognitiō, recognitiōnis, f.	*recognition*
stirps, stirpis, gen. pl., stirpium, f.	*thorn*
tigris, tigris, gen. pl., tigrium, m./f.	*tiger*

4th Declension:

cōnsēnsus, -ūs, m.	*agreement*
impetus, -ūs, m.	***attack***

ADJECTIVES:

1st and 2nd Declension:

bēstiārius, -a, -um	*involving wild beasts*
claudus, -a, -um	*lame*
exanimātus, -a, -um	*paralyzed*
mānsuētus, -a, -um	*tame*
mūtuus, -a, -um	***mutual***

3rd Declension:

immānis, -is, -e	***huge***
mīrābilis, -is, -e	*wonderful*
mītis, -is, -e	***gentle***

ADVERBS:

blandē	*in a coaxing/winning manner*
clēmenter	*in a kindly manner*
placidē	*gently, peacefully, quietly, tamely*
quasi	***as if***

VERBS:

1st Conjugation:

admīror, -ārī, -ātus sum	***to wonder (at)***
condemnō, -āre, -āvī, -ātus	*to condemn*
līberō, -āre, -āvī, -ātus	*to set free*
mīror, -ārī, -ātus sum	***to wonder***

2nd Conjugation:

doleō, -ēre, -uī, -itūrus	***to be sorry, be sad, be in pain***
lateō, -ēre, -uī	***to lie in hiding, hide***

3rd Conjugation: **cōgō, cōgere, coēgī, coāctus**   *to compel, force*
                     immittō, immittere, immīsī, immissus   *to send in, release*
                     intellegō, intellegere, intellēxī, intellēctus   *to understand, realize*
                     intrōdūcō, intrōdūcere, intrōdūxī, intrōductus   *to bring in*
                     lambō, lambere, lambī   *to lick*
                     parcō, parcere, pepercī + dat.   *to spare*
                     vēscor, vēscī + abl.   *to feed (on)*

3rd Conjugation (-iō):
                     incipiō, incipere, incēpī, inceptus   *to begin*

WORDS AND PHRASES: admīrātiōnī esse   *to be a source of amazement (to)*
                                       rē vērā   ***really, actually***
                                 redeāmus   *let us return*

Chapter 50

NOUNS:

1st Declension:

epulae, -ārum, f.	*banquet, feast*
nātūra, -ae, f.	*nature*
prōnuba, -ae, f.	*bride's attendant*
serva, -ae, f.	*slave-woman, slave-girl*
spōnsa, -ae, f.	*betrothed woman, bride*

2nd Declension:

ānulus, -ī, m.	*ring*
propinquus, -ī, m.	*relative*
spōnsus, -ī, m.	*betrothed man, bridegroom*

3rd Declension:

avis, avis, gen. pl., **avium,** m./f.	*bird*
gēns, gentis, gen. pl., **gentium,** f.	*family, clan*
iuvenis, iuvenis, m.	*young man*
sōl, sōlis, m.	*sun*
spōnsālia, spōnsālium, n. pl.	*betrothal ceremony*

ADJECTIVES:

1st and 2nd Declension:

conversus, -a, -um	*having turned, turning*
dēditus, -a, -um	*devoted, dedicated*
perturbātus, -a, -um	*confused*
serēnus, -a, -um	*clear, bright*
sinister, sinistra, sinistrum	*left*
submissus, -a, -um	*quiet, subdued, soft*

3rd Declension:

nōbilis, -is, -e	*noble*
similis, -is, -e + gen. or dat.	*similar (to), like*

ADVERBS:

adeō	*so, so much, to such an extent*
nūper	*recently*

CONJUNCTIONS:

ut	*that (introducing result clauses)*
ut...nōn	*that...not (introducing negative result clauses)*

INTERJECTION:

Heus!	*Hey there!*

VERBS:

1st Conjugation:

aptō, -āre, -āvī, -ātus	*to place, fit*
grātulor, -ārī, -ātus sum + dat.	*to congratulate*
observō, -āre, -āvī, -ātus	*to watch, pay attention to*

2nd Conjugation:

decet, decēre, decuit	*it is right, proper, fitting*
dēspondeō, dēspondēre, dēspondī, dēspōnsus	*to betroth, promise in marriage*
lūcet, lūcēre, lūxit	*it is light, it is day; (it) shines*

oportet, oportēre, oportuit	*it is right, fitting; ought*
spondeō, spondēre, spopondī, spōnsus	*to promise solemnly, pledge*
taedet, taedēre, taesum est	*boredom with/weariness of something* (gen.) *affects one* (acc.), *one is bored with, weary of something*

3rd Conjugation:

dēmittō, dēmittere, dēmīsī, dēmissus	*to let down, lower*
neglegō, neglegere, neglēxī, neglēctus	*to neglect, ignore*
rescrībō, rescrībere, rescrīpsī, rescrīptus	*to write back, reply*

WORDS AND PHRASES:

ad spōnsālia	*for the betrothal*
ait	*(he/she) says, said*
cūrae esse	*to be a cause of anxiety (to)*
Festināre tē oportet	*That you hurry is fitting, You ought to hurry*
in mātrimōnium dūcere	*to marry*
lūcēbat	*(it) was shining*
Mē taedet sōlitūdinis	*Boredom with/Weariness of solitude affects me, I am bored with/weary of solitude*
Nōn decet patrem dēspondēre fīliam	*That a father should betroth his daughter is not fitting, It is not fitting for a father to betroth his daughter*

Chapter 51

NOUNS:

1st Declension:

benevolentia, -ae, f.	*kindness*
bulla, -ae, f.	*luck-charm, locket*
familia, -ae, f.	*family, household*
tabulae, -ārum, f. pl.	*tablets, records*

2nd Declension:

ātrium, -ī, n.	*atrium, main room*
larārium, -ī, n.	*shrine of the household gods*
officium, -ī, n.	*official ceremony, duty*
Tabulārium, -ī, n.	*Public Records Office*

3rd Declension:

Larēs, Larum, m. pl.	*household gods*
Līberālia, Līberālium, n. pl.	*the Liberalia (Festival of Liber)*
līmen, līminis, n.	**threshold, doorway**

ADJECTIVES:

1st and 2nd Declension:

nōnnūllī, -ae, -a	*some*
pūblicus, -a, -um	*public*
pūrus, -a, -um	**spotless, clean, plain white**

3rd Declension:

familiāris, -is, -e	**belonging to the family/ household**
puerīlis, -is, -e	*childish, of childhood*

CONJUNCTIONS:

nē	**not to (introducing indirect commands)**
ut	**to (introducing indirect commands)**

PREPOSITION:

ergā + acc.	*toward*

VERBS:

1st Conjugation:

comitor, -ārī, -ātus sum	**to accompany**
cōnsecrō, -āre, -āvī, -ātus	*to dedicate*
hortor, -ārī, -ātus sum	**to encourage, urge**
imperō, -āre, -āvī, -ātus + dat.	**to order**
ōrō, -āre, -āvī, -ātus	**to beg**

3rd Conjugation:

amplector, amplectī, amplexus sum	**to embrace**
dēdūcō, dēdūcere, dēdūxī, dēductus	*to show into, bring, escort*
dīmittō, dīmittere, dīmīsī, dīmissus	**to send away**
īnscrībō, īnscrībere, īnscrīpsī, īnscrīptus	*to write in, register*
sūmō, sūmere, sūmpsī, sūmptus	**to take, take up, pick out, assume (i.e., put on for the first time)**

3rd Conjugation (-iō):

praecipiō, praecipere, praecēpī, praeceptus + dat.	**to instruct, order**

WORDS AND PHRASES:

erat īnscrībendum	*(it) had to be registered*
grātiās agere + dat.	***to thank***
in Forum dēdūcere	*to escort into the Forum*
invītāverat ut	*he had invited (them) to*
nē sē dīmitteret	*not to send them away*
officium togae virīlis	*coming of age ceremony*
sī quis	***if anyone***
toga praetexta, -ae, f.	*toga with purple border*
toga pūra, -ae, f.	*plain white toga*
toga virīlis, togae virīlis	*toga of manhood, plain white toga*

Chapter 52

NOUNS:

1st Declension:

caterva, -ae, f.	*crowd*
mātrōna, -ae, f.	*married woman*
prūdentia, -ae, f.	*good sense, discretion, skill*

2nd Declension:

cōnsultum, -ī, n.	*decree*
ingenium, -ī, n.	*intelligence, ingenuity*

3rd Declension:

cognōmen, cognōminis, n.	*surname (third name of a Roman)*
interrogātiō, interrogātiōnis, f.	*questioning*
mōs, mōris, m.	*custom,* pl., *character*
patrēs, patrum, m. pl.	*senators*

5th Declension:

fidēs, fideī, f.	*good faith, reliability, trust*

ADJECTIVES:

1st and 2nd Declension:

posterus, -a, -um	*next, following*
praetextātus, -a, -um	*wearing the* **toga praetexta**

3rd Declension:

trepidāns, trepidantis	*in a panic*

VERBS:

1st Conjugation:

ēnūntiō, -āre, -āvī, -ātus	*to reveal, divulge*

2nd Conjugation:

praebeō, -ēre, -uī, -itus	*to display, show, provide*
urgeō, urgēre, ursī	*to press, insist*

3rd Conjugation:

agō, agere, ēgī, āctus	*to do, drive; to discuss, debate*

Irregular:

introeō, introīre, introiī or introīvī, introitūrus	*to enter*
perferō, perferre, pertulī, perlātus	*to report*
prōferō, prōferre, prōtulī, prōlātus	*to carry forward, continue*

WORDS AND PHRASES:

dīxit āctum esse	*he said that there had been a debate*
eō magis	*all the more*
honōris causā	*for the sake of an honor, as an honor*
nē quis	*that no one*
placuit	*it was decided*
potius quam	*rather than*
utrum...an...	*whether...or...*

Chapter 53

NOUNS:

1st Declension:

āra, -ae, f.	*altar*
dextra, -ae, f.	*right hand*
exsequiae, -ārum, f. pl.	*funeral rites*
nūptiae, -ārum, f. pl.	*wedding ceremony*
taeda, -ae, f.	*torch*
vitta, -ae, f.	*ribbon*

2nd Declension:

concubīnus, -ī, m.	*bridegroom*
exta, -ōrum, n. pl.	*the inner organs of sacrificial animals (heart, lungs, liver)*
flammeum, -ī, n.	*orange (bridal) veil*
hortulus, -ī, m.	*small garden*
laurus, -ī, f.	*bay (tree), laurel*
marītus, -ī, m.	*husband*
modus, -ī, m.	*way, method, rhythmic/ harmonious manner*
mundus, -ī, m.	*articles used by a woman to beautify herself*
myrtus, -ī, f.	*myrtle*
Ōceanus, -ī, m.	*Ocean*
rēticulum, -ī, n.	*hairnet*
sacra, -ōrum, n. pl.	*religious rites, sacrifice*
Talassius, -ī, m.	*Talassius (god of marriage)*

3rd Declension:

auspex, auspicis, m.	*augur, officiating priest*
dēductiō, dēductiōnis, f.	*procession*
fax, facis, f.	*wedding-torch*
fūnus, fūneris, n.	*funeral*
haruspex, haruspicis, m.	*soothsayer, diviner*
hilaritās, hilaritātis, f.	*good humor, merriment, fun*
nux, nucis, f.	*nut*
ōmen, ōminis, n.	*omen*
pulchritūdō, pulchritūdinis, f.	*beauty*
viscera, viscerum, n. pl.	*vital organs*

ADJECTIVES:

1st and 2nd Declension:

albus, -a, -um	*white*
cārus, -a, -um	*dear, beloved*
castus, -a, -um	*virtuous, chaste*
clārus, -a, -um	*bright*
eximius, -a, -um	*outstanding*
hyacinthinus, -a, -um	*of hyacinth*
siccus, -a, -um	*dry*
varius, -a, -um	*different, various, varied, many-hued*

3rd Declension:	iners, inertis	*lazy*
	nūptiālis, -is, -e	*of/for a wedding*

ADVERBS:

	Fēlīciter!	*Good luck!*
	mortiferē	*mortally, critically*
	rīte	**properly**

CONJUNCTIONS:

	nē	***lest, so that...not, to avoid, to prevent (introducing negative purpose clauses)***
	ut	***to, so that (introducing purpose clauses)***

PREPOSITIONS:

	dē + abl.	***down from, from, concerning, about***
	super + acc.	*over, above*

INTERJECTIONS:

	Hymēn! / Hymenaee!	an exclamation chanted at weddings; later thought of as the god of weddings
	Iō!	a ritual exclamation

VERBS:

1st Conjugation:

	interrogō, -āre, -āvī, -ātus	*to ask*
	obsignō, -āre, -āvī, -ātus	*to sign*
	ōrnō, -āre, -āvī, -ātus	***to decorate***
	sacrificō, -āre, -āvī, -ātus	*to sacrifice*

2nd Conjugation:

	ārdeō, ārdēre, ārsī, ārsūrus	***to burn, blaze***
	fleō, flēre, flēvī, flētus	***to weep, cry***
	libet, libēre, libuit or **libitum est**	***it is pleasing to someone*** (dat.) ***to do something*** (infin.)

3rd Conjugation:

	compōnō, compōnere, composuī, compositus	*to compose*
	concinō, concinere, concinuī	*to sing together*
	dēcēdō, dēcēdere, dēcessī, dēcessūrus	***to die***
	dēsinō, dēsinere, dēsiī, dēsitus	***to stop***
	iungō, iungere, iūnxī, iūnctus	***to join***
	praecēdō, praecēdere, praecessī, praecessūrus	*to go in front*
	prōrumpō, prōrumpere, prōrūpī, prōruptus	*to burst forth, burst out*

4th Conjugation:

	operiō, operīre, operuī, opertus	***to hide, cover***
	serviō, -īre, -īvī, -ītūrus + dat.	***to serve***

Irregular:

	prōdeō, prōdīre, prōdiī, prōditūrus	*to come forth*

WORDS AND PHRASES:

dūxit exsequiās	*(he/she) carried out the funeral rites*
mundus muliebris	*jewelry, perfumes, toilet articles, and attire of the grown-up woman*
nova nūpta, -ae, f.	*bride*
super līmen tollere	*to carry over the threshold*
tabulās nūptiālēs obsignāre	*to sign the marriage contract*
tunica alba, -ae, f.	*white tunic (worn by brides)*

Chapter 54

NOUNS:

1st Declension:

candēla, -ae, f.	*candle*
coxa, -ae, f.	*hipbone*
fortūna, -ae, f.	*fortune (good or bad)*
harēna, -ae, f.	*sand*
īnferiae, -ārum, f. pl.	*offerings and rites in honor of the dead at the tomb*
līberta, -ae, f.	*freedwoman*
lucerna, -ae, f.	*lamp*
nēnia, -ae, f.	*lament, dirge*
pompa, -ae, f.	*procession*
vīta, -ae, f.	*life*

2nd Declension:

capillī, -ōrum, m. pl.	*hair*
īnferī, -ōrum, m. pl.	*the underworld, the gods of the underworld*
meritum, -ī, n.	*good deed*; pl., *services*
mīmus, -ī, m.	*actor of mime, buffoon*
monumentum, -ī, n.	*monument, tomb*
morbus, -ī, m.	***illness***
nātus, -ī, m.	***son***
rogus, -ī, m.	*funeral pyre*

3rd Declension:

āctor, āctōris, m.	*actor*
aequor, aequoris, n.	*sea*
appāritor, appārtōris, m.	*public servant*
aquilō, aquilōnis, m.	*north wind*
cinis, cineris, m.	***ashes, dust (of the cremated body)***
cor, cordis, n.	***heart***
familiārēs, familiārium, m. pl.	***members of the household***
fascēs, fascium, m. pl.	*rods (symbols of office)*
febris, febris, gen. pl., febrium, f.	*fever*
gēns, gentis, gen. pl., gentium, f.	***family, clan***; pl., ***peoples***
imāgō, imāginis, f.	***likeness, mask***
laudātiō, laudātiōnis, f.	*speech of praise*
līctor, līctōris, m.	*lictor, officer*
maiōrēs, maiōrum, m. pl.	***ancestors***
manēs, manium, m. pl.	*spirits of the dead*
mūnus, mūneris, n.	***gift, service, gladiatorial show***; pl., ***games***
os, ossis, n.	*bone*
pectus, pectoris, n.	*chest, breast*
pīstor, pīstōris, m.	*baker*
redēmptor, redēmptōris, m.	*contractor*
sermō, sermōnis, m.	***conversation, talk***
tībīcen, tībīcinis, m.	*piper*
vispillō, vispillōnis, m.	*undertaker*

| **4th Declension:** | **flētus, -ūs,** m. | *weeping, tears* |
| | incessus, -ūs, m. | bearing, walk(ing) |

ADJECTIVES:
1st and 2nd Declension:

	comitātus, -a, -um	*accompanied*
	commodus, -a, -um	*pleasant*
	frāternus, -a, -um	*brotherly*
	gelātus, -a, -um	*chilled*
	grātus, -a, -um	*loved (by), pleasing (to), dear (to)*
	iūcundus, -a, -um	*pleasant, delightful*
	lepidus, -a, -um	*charming*
	lūbricus, -a, -um	*slippery*
	mūtus, -a, -um	*silent*
	officiōsus, -a, -um + dat.	*ready to serve, obliging*
	paul(l)us, -a, -um	*little, small*
	perpetuus, -a, -um	*lasting, permanent*
	prīscus, -a, -um	*of olden times, ancient*
	situs, -a, -um	*located, situated, buried*
	subitus, -a, -um	*sudden*
	vectus, -a, -um,	*having been carried, having traveled*

3rd Declension:

	fūnebris, -is, -e	*funeral*
	hilaris, -is, -e	*cheerful*
	levis, -is, -e	*light*
	lēvis, -is, -e	*smooth*
	mollis, -is, -e	*soft*

PRONOUN:

| | tētē | emphatic **tē** |

ADVERBS:

	indignē	*undeservedly*
	nēquīquam	*in vain*
	prōtinus	*immediately*

CONJUNCTIONS:

| | quandōquidem | *since* |
| | **ut** | *as, when* |

VERBS:
1st Conjugation:

	adstō, adstāre, adstitī	*to stand near, stand by*
	commemorō, -āre, -āvī, -ātus	*to mention, comment on, recount*
	creō, -āre, -āvī, -ātus	*to appoint, create*
	dōnō, -āre, -āvī, -ātus	*to give; to present somebody* (acc.) *with something* (abl.)
	locō, -āre, -āvī, -ātus	*to place*
	mānō, -āre, -āvī	*to flow*
	nōminō, -āre, -āvī, -ātus	*to name, call by name*
	optō, -āre, -āvī, -ātus	*to wish*
	plōrō, -āre, -āvī, -ātus	*to lament, mourn*
	violō, -āre, -āvī,-ātus	*to do harm, harm*

2nd Conjugation:	langueō, languēre	*to be ill in bed*

3rd Conjugation:

accendō, accendere, accendī, accēnsus	*to set on fire*
alloquor, alloquī, allocūtus sum	*to speak to, address*
āvertō, āvertere, āvertī, āversus	*to turn away, divert*
dīligō, dīligere, dīlēxī, dīlēctus	*to love, have special regard for*
ēruō, ēruere, ēruī, ērutus	*to dig up*
excēdō, excēdere, excessī, excessūrus	*to go out, leave*
eximō, eximere, exēmī, exēmptus	*to remove*
exstruō, exstruere, exstrūxī, exstrūctus	*to build*
frangō, frangere, frēgī, frāctus	*to break*
impōnō, impōnere, imposuī, impositus	*to place on, put*
incidō, incidere, incidī, incāsūrus	*to fall into/onto*
ingravēscō, ingravēscere	*to grow worse*
linquō, linquere, līquī	*to leave*
perlegō, perlegere, perlēgī, perlēctus	*to read through*
plangō, plangere, plānxī, plānctus	*to beat*
requīrō, requīrere, requīsīvī, requīsītus	*to ask, inquire*
scindō, scindere, scidī, scissus	*to cut, split, carve, tear*
solvō, solvere, solvī, solūtus	*to loosen, untie, dishevel*
tangō, tangere, tetigī, tāctus	*to touch*
tegō, tegere, tēxī, tēctus	*to cover*
vehō, vehere, vexī, vectus	*to carry;* pass., *to be carried, travel*

3rd Conjugation (iō):		
	afficiō, afficere, affēcī, affectus	*to affect*
	iniciō, inicere, iniēcī, iniectus	*to throw into, thrust into*
	recipiō, recipere, recēpī, receptus	*to receive, recapture*

Irregular:	cōnferō, cōnferre, contulī, collātus	*to confer, bestow*

WORDS AND PHRASES:

aquilōne gelātae	*chilled by the north wind*
capillīs solūtīs	*with dishevelled hair*
dīs mānibus	*to the spirits of the dead*
ē vītā excēdere	*to die*
est arcessendus	*(he) must be sent for*
in perpetuum	*forever*
lōtus est	*he bathed*
merita cōnferre	*to render services (to)*
pectus plangere	*to beat the breast*
scissā veste	*with torn clothing*
sit	*may it be*
Via Flāminia, -ae, f.	*Via Flaminia (a road from Rome leading through the Campus Martius and north to Ariminum on the Adriatic Sea)*